Headwaters Bible Curriculum

Part 1: Old Testament

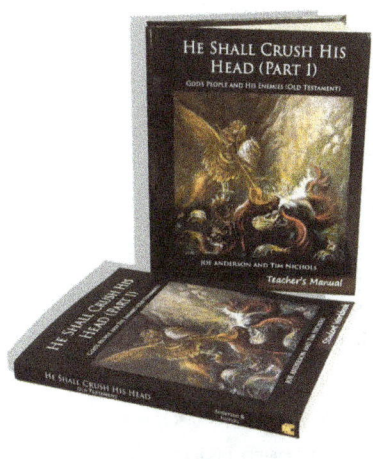

Grade level: 6 7 8 9 | 10 11 12

God made the world for us to govern and guard, hand in hand with Him. We wrecked it, but God never gave up on us. Too often glossed over, the Old Testament Story lays a fundamental understanding of who God is and how He relates to His people — and without this story, Jesus makes no sense. Begin at the beginning and give your students a strong foundation.

Part 2: New Testament

Grade level: 6 | 7 8 9 10 | 11 12

Jesus was exactly who the prophets foretold, in a way that surprised everyone. With the Old Testament Story as context, let your students experience the surprise of Jesus. Let them see how He lived as God's incarnate love, how He gave Himself for us, how He sent twelve guys to turn the world upside down — and how He is sending us to continue their work.

Part 3: The Path of the Wise

Grade level: 6 | 7 8 9 10 11 12

Our Priest, King, and Prophet, Jesus of Nazareth, delivered us from sin and death to follow Him, to be His Body in the world. Challenge your students to follow Jesus: as a priest, presenting the world to God; as king, navigating conflict in a Christlike way; as prophet, learning to hear God well and carry His message to the world.

Copyright © 2015 by Tim Nichols

All rights reserved
Printed in the United States of America
First Edition

No part of this book may be reproduced in any form or by any electronic or mechanical means, including information storage and retrieval systems, except for brief quotations in printed reviews, without the prior permission of the author.

Unless otherwise indicated, all Scripture quotations are taken from the New King James Version®. Copyright © 1982 by Thomas Nelson, Inc. Used by permission. All rights reserved.

Scripture quotations marked (NIV) are taken from the Holy Bible, New International Version®, NIV®. Copyright © 1973, 1978, 1984, 2011 by Biblica, Inc.™ Used by permission of Zondervan. All rights reserved worldwide. www.zondervan.com The "NIV" and "New International Version" are trademarks registered in the United States Patent and Trademark Office by Biblica, Inc.™

Author's translation or paraphrase indicated by an asterisk after the reference.

ISBN: 978-1-945413-90-2

Table of Contents

Introduction ... 4
Lesson 1 Start with God's Word ... 9
Lesson 2 Without Excuse ... 17
Lesson 3 Don't Get Robbed! ... 25
Lesson 4 Answer a Fool ... 33
Lesson 5 Loving the Different ... 39
Lesson 6 Growing to Maturity ... 47
Lesson 7 Living in Beauty ... 55

Introduction

In the field of Christian apologetics, we've had several decades dominated by the impulse to love God with all our minds. We've raised up a generation of young Christians with eagle eyes for poor reasoning and lack of evidence, and that is all to the good. But in our zeal to attend to the intellectual concerns, we have missed a deeper issue. Poor reasoning and lack of evidence are common among those who despise Christ, even among those who have really thought about it; but Scripture makes it clear that faulty reasoning is not *why* they despise Christ in the first place. In fact, God tells us that they hate Him for quite different reasons. The intellectual weapons of unbelief are not the roots of unbelief; rather they are excuses invented after the fact, decoys used to keep the real issues from surfacing.

In other words, we have focused on parrying the unbeliever's weapon and failed to go for his heart. In an apologetic discussion, courtesy requires us to respond to the unbeliever's arguments seriously, but faithfulness to Scripture requires that we never get distracted by excuses for unbelief. Whatever excuses the unbeliever offers for his unbelief, we want to respond in such a way that we expose the excuses for what they are in order to move the conversation toward the heart of the matter. The first principle of winning apologetics is to trust what God says —about the unbeliever's heart and our own— and apply it.

In this book, you will find a different approach to apologetics, one that is founded on Scripture itself. This biblical approach allows for a kind of "zone defense" against the intellectual attacks of unbelievers, and at the same time provides us with a means to exploit those attacks to get to the heart of the matter.

In order to prepare for a conversation that can get to the heart of the matter, we need to lay a foundation in our own hearts first, and it must be the foundation that God has given us. "Unless the Lord builds the house, they labor in vain that build it." The Devotional Apologetics house has two major parts: the Support Structure and the Upper Room. The Support Structure is made up of the key biblical insights and commitments that give us a spiritual and conceptual understanding of what's happening in the conversation. What we learn about unbelief in the Support Structure lessons will also help us to guard our own hearts from being seduced by unbelieving thought. It's easier to get trapped than you might think.

Useful as it is, if we remain at the level of the Support Structure, all we're going to do is win arguments. In order to win hearts, we move into the Upper Room. The Upper Room rests on the foundation of key biblical truths in the Support Structure, but moves from just defending the faith to launching an offense that matters. In the Upper Room, we will introduce students to three key ways of understanding and living the biblical Story that will help their unbelieving friends to meet God through them. As we live out the implications of the Story, we will be able to invite unbelievers into the family of God in such a way that they actually want to join it.

The Support Structure

The Support Structure is a set of four lessons drawn from four key biblical passages. The first three lessons focus on getting our own hearts right before God and clarifying our own understanding regarding what Scripture says about unbelief. We will look at some sample arguments in those lessons, but mostly for the purpose of illustrating the temptations of an apologetic discussion and exploring how our own hearts can go wrong. The fourth Support Structure lesson addresses the key biblical principle that governs how to actually talk with an unbeliever.

We will begin, as we should, at the beginning. In Genesis 1-3 we find the foundation for understanding how unbelief works. Adam and Eve made a pair of critical mistakes. Every unbeliever since has followed in their footsteps--and we are not immune to those same temptations. In fact, anytime we feel like an unbeliever has made a really strong argument, we are succumbing to at least one of these two temptations, and we have the opportunity to repent.

From there, we will move into Romans 1, where Paul explains that God made everything in order to clearly communicate the truth about Himself. This means that unbelief is never simply ignorant; it is foolish. The unbeliever knows God all right—he just doesn't like Him. Then he bolsters that dislike by believing lies about God. So we are not simply on a mission to educate; we are on a mission to call a God-hating pagan to repentance, to minister the love of Christ to a heart that hates God. Along the way, we are also going to clear up some lies about who God is.

As he meditates on the sufficiency of Christ in his letter to the Colossian church, Paul says that all the treasures of wisdom and knowledge are hidden in Him, and this gives us our third crucial element for understanding apologetic conversations. All the facts worth knowing and all the skills worth having are in Christ; anybody who has any of them got them from Christ, whether he admits it or not. We often cannot see how this is the case, but at those very moments the apologetic encounter becomes a great opportunity for our own sanctification and growth. If we ask God to show us how He sees the issue at hand, He will guide us. If we fail to believe what Paul said, then we will get spiritually robbed.

The final element of the Support Structure is the standard for our speech. When the unbeliever refuses to take God seriously—as all unbelievers do—he is being a fool, and Proverbs 26:4-5 gives us the biblical standards for speaking to a fool. Answering the argument is the way of the debater, but God has a much higher calling for us. God calls us to answer the *person* without descending to his level, to speak to him in such a way that his own folly is evident to him.

Key resources for the Support Structure

1. The Bahnsen/Stein Debate
In 1985, the University of California at Irvine hosted a debate between Christian philosopher and apologist Greg Bahnsen and Gordon Stein. While he had no formal philosophical training, Dr. Stein was a noted expert on hoaxes and spiritualism and a vocal opponent of religion in all its forms. The debate remains one of the clearest demonstrations on record of Bahnsen's non-traditional approach to defending the Christian faith.

Audio of the debate is available from Covenant Media Foundation and in various places online, and transcripts are also available. We recommend you have transcripts available for reading or following along with the audio.

2. *Collision* DVD
In 2008, *Christianity Today* hosted a debate on their website on the question, "Is Christianity good for the world?" Each of the two parties—atheist and moralist Christopher Hitchens and pastor and author Doug Wilson—contributed

a series of articles. That article series was so popular that it became a book, and the publisher wanted to do a book tour. Neither of the authors wanted to spend days sitting at tables signing books, so they did a debate tour instead. Meeting in colleges, churches, and even a famous pub in Georgetown, Wilson and Hitchens debated the issues in a number of cities.

A film crew went with them, and *Collision* is the resulting documentary, endorsed by both Wilson and Hitchens as a fair representation of their views. In it, viewers have the opportunity to meet the men, observe some of their private conversations between debates, and see the debates themselves.

We highly recommend that you take the time to show this DVD in the classroom. Wilson presents a model of Christian civility and charity throughout his contact with Hitchens, while never backing down on his Christian witness. You can buy the DVD from Canon Press or a number of retail outlets online.

Additional Resources for the Support Structure

- Charles Clough, "Why I Believe in God" (2 lectures, available from bibleframework.com)
- James Nickel, *Mathematics: Is God Silent?*
- J. Budziszewski, *What We Can't Not Know*
- Rousas John Rushdoony, *The One and the Many*
- Greg Bahnsen, *Pushing the Antithesis*

The Upper Room

The Upper Room has three key elements, but they're really just three different ways of telling the same Story. Once we understand the truths of the Support Structure, we know that all we're really doing in evangelism is inviting unbelievers to live in the real world...and admit it. But doing that winsomely requires some angle of approach, and these three have proven particularly helpful.

It's important to emphasize to your students that there is only one Story. Like a diamond, the Story has many facets, and you can't see all the facets at once. You can turn the stone and turn it, and look at it from all different angles. From any given angle, your perspective is limited to the facets you can see, but the light and the fire that you see from your particular angle of view also depends on those unseen facets, and in that way, you do see evidence of all the facets from any direction you care to look. In the same way, these three tellings of the Story are just three of an infinite number of tellings, three different ways of turning the diamond. While they emphasize certain things and leave other things in the background, the whole Story is always there.

The Story is a love story. It begins in eternity past, with the three different Persons of the Triune God. The Father loves the Son and the Spirit, the Son loves the Father and the Spirit, and the Spirit loves the Father and the Son—eternally. At a certain point, God chose to make a self-portrait and created the universe, which represents certain key truths about God. Within that universe, He placed humanity as His special self-portrait...but we failed to live up to our calling, with disastrous consequences for ourselves and the world. In love, God took the cost of our failure upon Himself, achieved victory over our failure, and is in the process of sharing that victory with us. In the end, love conquers all, and we become what we were always meant to be—the loving image of a loving God.

The Story is a coming-of-age story. It begins with God our Father lovingly choosing to have children—Adam and Eve. In our infancy in the garden, we utterly failed to follow our Father's instructions, and we broke the world and caused all kinds of problems. Slowly but surely, though, God is growing the human race into maturity. As the gospel of Jesus Christ sinks into human societies, the problems that have plagued us slowly abate, and one day, the knowledge of the glory of Yahweh will cover the earth like water covers the sea. On that day, Christ will triumph, we will finally be grown up, and the problems of sin and its results will be solved.

The Story is beautiful. It is the tale of a beautiful God who made a beautiful creation in His image—the ultimate mixed-media piece—only to have us introduce ugliness and futility into it. A fearful god would simply have walked away from it all. An angry god would have just destroyed us all. But our God...He entered into His wrecked work of art and transformed it into something even more beautiful. As the Story gets into your guts, you will begin to live beautifully. Many people feel themselves trapped in a life of hopeless ugliness, and as you live beautifully in front of them, they will be attracted to the life you have.

Key Resources for the Upper Room

1. N. D. Wilson, *Notes from the Tilt-a-Whirl* (book and DVD)
2. Richard Bledsoe, *Can Saul Alinsky be Saved?*

Devotional Apologetics Project

If you want a larger project that spans the entire series of lessons, here is a project you can use:

Have your students choose an atheist resource. Christopher Hitchens' series of articles under the title "Is Christianity Good for the World?" or his book "God is Not Great" would be good choices, and resources are plentiful online as well. We suggest you pre-approve what your students use, just to make sure it's a big enough resource to be worth doing the work in the project below.

Have them engage their chosen resource in three different ways.

1. Summarize the unbelievers' arguments. Be fair and respectful. Summarize the argument in such a way that the author would be able to look at it and say, "Yes, that's what I said." It does no good to refute an unbeliever's argument if he doesn't recognize his own position in the argument you're refuting. This portion of the project can be due anytime during the Support Structure lessons.

2. Find and expose the foolishness in the unbelievers' arguments. Without being insulting or demeaning, state the foolishness as starkly as possible. At this stage, we are looking for logical contradictions, arbitrary appeals to authority, and stolen capital. "By what standard?" will be an important question throughout the assignment. Assign this portion of the project after the students have completed the Support Structure lessons.

3. Make a positive counter-argument by showing the value and beauty of the Christian way of understanding the world. Include actions you might take as well as things you can say. Speaking has its place, but sometimes the best argument is a small, kind action, a prayer, a smile on a bad day. Assign this portion of the project after the students have completed the Upper Room lessons.

The Apologetics House

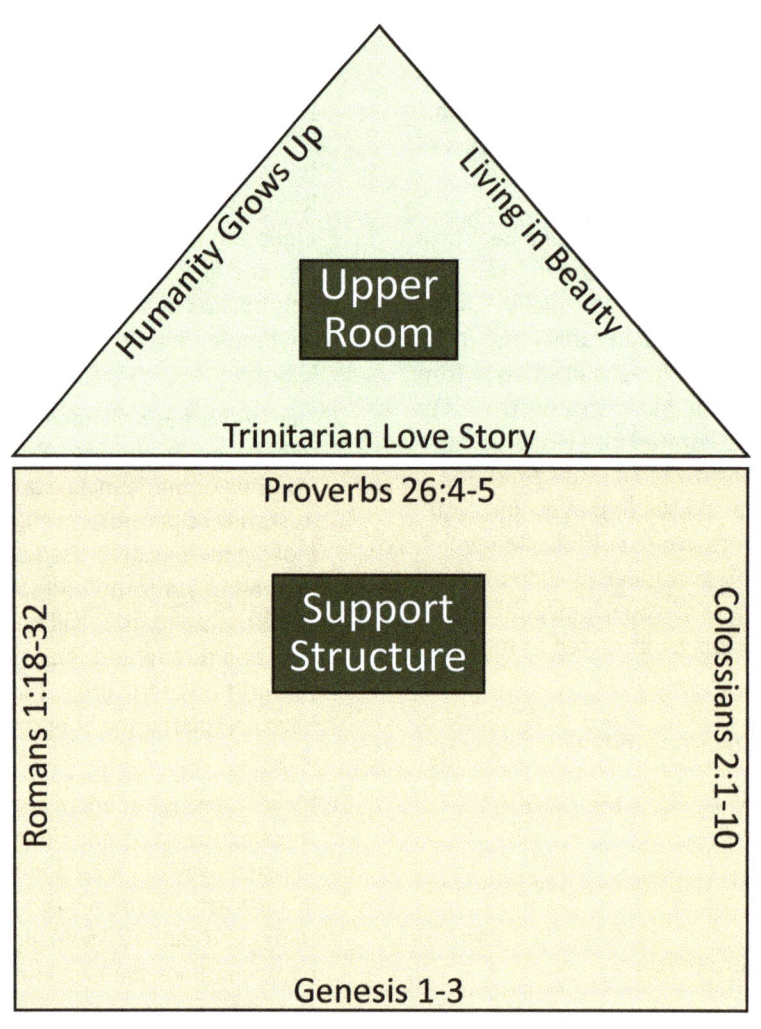

LESSON 1

Devotional Apologetics: Start with God's Word

NOTES TO THE TEACHER

This is the first of four Support Structure lessons. For more information on how these four lessons relate to each other—and to the three Upper Room Discourse lessons that will follow—please see the introduction.

The sunset puzzle
As the setting sun paints the sky red and gold, two people sit on a hill in the evening, watching the sunset. One of them, a Christian, says, "Wow! God is amazing!" The other one, an atheist, looks at his friend in disbelief. "Where'd you get that from?" he says. "All I see are molecules in motion. But they are pretty." This situation presents us with the central problem in apologetics: how is it possible that two people can look at the same sunset and see such different things? When we understand the Bible's answer to that question, we will have a solid foundation for understanding apologetics.

The foundation for apologetics must begin at the beginning. The world is God's. He made it for us and us for it. We are designed and commissioned to lovingly guard and cultivate the world as God's representatives, but we are meant to do this in communion with Him. He talks with us and walks with us, from the very beginning. Because the world is God's, because He made it and us, it is not possible for us to take a neutral stance toward God. We *owe* Him, from the very beginning. We have a duty to say "Thank you," and mean it, and live in a grateful way.

OVERVIEW

As with any other issue in Scripture, it is best in apologetics to begin at the beginning. By looking at the very beginning of human history with apologetics in mind, we learn about the key temptations that are at the very core of apologetics. These temptations are the same for believers and unbelievers, and we must learn to defeat them in our own hearts before we will be ready to address them in anyone else.

SOURCE MATERIAL

- Genesis 1-3
- Isaiah 55:10-11

The Adam Mistake
Every human being is turned loose in God's world, and living before God in His world, there are two basic errors a human being can make. The story of the fall in Genesis 3 gives us both of these mistakes. The first error is the Adam Mistake—Adam understood very clearly that he was not supposed to eat the fruit, and he ate it anyway. Adam's error was straightforward rebellion, choosing to be a god unto himself rather than accepting his place in creation as God's chosen representative. The ingratitude in the Adam Mistake is obvious. God literally gave Adam the whole world, and he had to go grabbing for the one thing God told him to leave alone.

Devotional Apologetics

> **OBJECTIVES**
>
> **The student will feel...**
>
> - the allure of appealing to the unbeliever's ultimate authority.
> - the strain of trying to remain faithful to his own ultimate authority.
> - encouraged to use Scripture whether the unbeliever believes in it or not.
>
> **The student will understand...**
>
> - the nature of the Adam Mistake and the Eve Mistake.
> - how to avoid the Eve Mistake.
> - that ultimate authorities must be self-justifying.
> - that God's Word works whether people initially believe in it or not.
>
> **The student will apply this understanding by...**
>
> - practicing sticking to his ultimate authority under pressure.
> - reflecting on how his personal relationship with God is challenged when he sticks to the authority of God's Word.

The Eve Mistake—excluding God from the conversation
The Eve Mistake is a different sort of ingratitude and a little harder to get a handle on. In order to grasp it, we need to take a careful look at how the serpent tempted Eve, and there are two key stages to the temptation. The first is to *enter into a conversation that excludes God*. The serpent did this by asking a question, "Has God really said you can't eat from *any* tree in the garden?" Eve corrected him, but do you see what had already happened? Instead of being in a conversation *with* God, now Eve was in a conversation *about* God—a conversation that the devil was more than happy to direct. Imagine if right from the beginning, Eve had said, "Hold that thought, snakey—Hey, God! The snake's got a question for you...."

The Eve Mistake—"neutrality" toward God
Once he had Eve drawn into the conversation, the snake moved in for the kill. The way he started the conversation induced her to think that God was being stingy. "Has God *really* told you that you can't eat from *any* of these beautiful trees?" No, Eve said, just the one. She would die if she ate (or even touched) the fruit on that tree. At this point, Eve was ready to hear the lie, and the serpent was happy to provide it. "You will not die—God just knows that the minute you eat that fruit, your eyes will be opened, and you'll be like Him, knowing good and evil." Now comes the second stage of the temptation: *Eve adopted a neutral stance toward God*. She had two competing claims before her: would the fruit kill her, or would it make her like God?

Eve already knew that she had been created by God, given the world by God, given the fruit of every other tree in the garden by God. What would it look like for her to just be grateful for what she had? "You know, snakey, God's done an awful lot for me, and if He wanted to keep that one tree for Himself, that's His business. Everything He's done for me so far has been good, so I think I'll just trust Him with this one."

But what was Eve's thought process at this point? "So when the woman saw that the tree was good for food, and pleasant to the eyes, and a tree desirable to make one wise, she took its fruit and ate" (Gen 3:6).

Let's think about the factors that influenced Eve's decision. "Pleasant to the eyes" is easy—that's a straightforward sensory experience. "Good for food" is harder—how could she know that if she'd never tasted it? The answer is induction: she had tasted a lot of the other fruit in the garden, and this fruit resembled that fruit. Now where did she get the idea that it was "a tree desirable to make one wise"? From the snake.

So the fatal cocktail for the Eve Mistake looks like this: first, exclude God from the conversation. Second, try to assume a "neutral" footing and evaluate the world independently of God's input...and down you go, with the devil lying to you to help you along.

If Eve had kept in mind what God had said to her, the result could have been very different. "If you eat it, you'll die" + "It looks good" + "It seems like it would be good to eat" leads to "Thank you, God, for warning me not to eat that. Left to myself, I would have eaten it." But she lost track of God's warning, and on "neutral" ground, she was ripe for the devil's lie. She ate the fruit and died.

No neutrality possible
The Eve Mistake is *the* signal mistake that we make in apologetics as Christians. In the name of being "fair," we set aside God's Word and try to begin from "neutral" ground with an unbeliever. This is hard for us to avoid because it seems like civility and effectiveness in argument requires us to adopt a neutral stance, but that's not how relationships work. It's a matter of faithfulness to our relationship with God that we not pretend that there is any neutral ground.

Example: Did Jesus ever exist?
Let's look at how avoiding the Eve Mistake works out in practice. Suppose an unbeliever begins by saying "There's no evidence that Jesus ever lived." (Activity 1 addresses this issue—you may want to have the students engage the activity first and then teach it afterwards.)

Our first impulse is to seek out a birth announcement in the Bethlehem Times (if we could find one!), but we are *Christians*. We believe the Bible is the authority, so why wouldn't we begin by saying, "Matthew, Mark, Luke and John all provide records of Jesus' life."

Of course the unbeliever will object that he's not going to let us try to prove Christianity using the Bible. "That's circular reasoning!" he will say, *and he'll be right*. But there's a little more to it than that, so before we talk about what to say next, let's think a little more deeply about what's actually going on at the heart level at this point in the discussion.

The nature of ultimate authority
As Christians, we appeal to the Bible first of all because it is the Word of God, and God is the ultimate authority. What the unbeliever will invite you to do is first prove the Word of God is true based on some *other* authority that *he* accepts as ultimate—and this is precisely what we must not do. Why not? Because you can't demonstrate that the Word of God is the *ultimate* authority by appealing to another authority. An ultimate authority, by its very nature, must be self-justifying. This is a kind of circular reasoning that is inevitable, and everybody has it.

Consider this (imaginary) example:

> Suppose the unbeliever says to you, "Look, there's no God. Science is the ultimate authority."

"How do you know?" you say.

"One day when I was sitting at the park under a willow tree," the unbeliever says, "an angel appeared to me and revealed to me that I can only really know something that is scientifically proven."

Do you see the problem? He is claiming science for his ultimate authority, but when pressed, he appeals to a scientifically unverifiable mystical experience to justify science as his authority... which means his mystical experience is his *real* ultimate authority. It isn't possible to justify your ultimate authority with appeals to other authorities. Real ultimate authority has to be self-justifying.

So an atheist will seek to bolster his position with science, and when the intelligent design folks come along and argue that the world was created, the atheist will say (as Dawkins, et al. often have) that intelligent design isn't science. Nothing but material explanations are allowed in science, and then materialistic science is used to bolster atheism, which in turn is used to justify materialistic science—and around we go. Everybody has this kind of circularity.

So when the unbeliever invites you to come to a "neutral" stance and prove your ultimate authority to him based on some other standard... that's not neutral at all. In fact, you're giving up God's Word as your ultimate authority and replacing it with his standard, whatever it might happen to be. He'll make it sound good—logic, reason, science, history and so on—but what's really happening is this: the unbeliever is asking you to give up your gratitude to God and accept unaided human reason as the ultimate authority—*which is the Eve Mistake all over again*. You must not do this, and you must not concede that it's okay for him to do it. It is not.

So what do you say? You point out that he is appealing to a different ultimate authority and challenge him to justify his. Whether he is willing to do it at this point doesn't really matter—the important thing is getting the issue of ultimate authority on the table.

Once that issue is on the table, though, you have a serious practical problem. If you and the unbeliever each have different ultimate authorities, and neither of you is willing to surrender your ultimate authority, how do you proceed? That's a good question, and we'll be addressing it in more detail in the coming lessons. For now, though, let's look at what happens if you simply continue to use the Bible. As Christians, we tend to assume that nothing will happen—the unbeliever does not recognize the authority of the Bible, so appealing to it will not help us win the argument. Stalemate.

Using the Bible
But don't forget, we aren't trying to win *the argument*. We are trying to win *the person*, and that calls for a different approach. Think of it this way—suppose you are walking down a dark city street and are cornered by a mugger. Suppose you have a pistol, which you draw and point at him. He begins laughing at you. "Sorry," he says between giggles, "but I don't believe in guns." Will his unbelief keep the gun from working? Of course not. So the real question is, will you let his unbelief keep you from *using* the gun? Of course not—but that's exactly what we do with the Bible.

Hebrews 4:12 tells us that the Word of God is a sword. So you're standing there holding your sword, and the unbeliever says to you,

"That's not a sword! In fact, I don't even believe in swords!" Now you can stand there with your sword in your hand and argue all day about whether it's really a sword or not. You can produce a ton of documentation on the definition of a sword and the characteristics of a sword and how this sword, right here, meets the definition and has all the characteristics.

Or you could just cut him with it.

The unbeliever does not believe that the Scriptures can do anything at all—but will that stop God's Word from being effective? Of course not. So why would we let his unbelief stop us from continuing to use it? "For as the rain comes down, and the snow from heaven, and do not return there, but water the earth and make it bring forth and bud, that it may give seed to the sower and bread to the eater—so shall My word be that goes forth from My mouth; it shall not return to Me void, but it shall accomplish what I please, and it shall prosper in the thing for which I sent it" (Isa 55:10-11).

The key phrase of this verse is "the thing for which I sent it." You can't just quote a verse and win the argument. The Scriptures weren't written to win arguments, but to win *people*. The Word of God does not serve *your* agenda. You can be certain, however, that if you bring the unbeliever into contact with the Scriptures, God's Word will do to his unbelieving heart what God sent it to do—it will cut him to the heart. The question is, do you trust God enough to use His Word, even though your unbelieving friend doesn't believe in it?

TEACHING OUTLINE

I. Introduction and review

   A. Teacher begins class by leading them in the Lord's Prayer: **"Our Father, who art in heaven, hallowed be Thy name. Thy kingdom come. Thy will be done on earth as it is in heaven. Give us this day our daily bread, and forgive us our trespasses, as we forgive those who trespass against us. And lead us not into temptation, but deliver us from evil. For Thine is the kingdom, and the power, and the glory forever and ever. Amen."**

   B. Today's place on the path: We're looking more deeply into how to defend the Christian faith in a way that is winning and faithful.

II. Today's lesson

   A. Introduction: the sunset puzzle

   B. Starting at the beginning

      1. Creation

      2. The Adam Mistake

      3. The Eve Mistake

      4. No neutrality possible

Devotional Apologetics

    C. Example: "There's no evidence Jesus ever lived."

        1. Ultimate authority

            a. Using the gospels

            b. "You can't use the Bible to prove the Bible."

            c. Thinking it through: circularity, ultimate authority and "neutrality"

        2. "But I don't believe the Bible."

            a. The mugger who doesn't believe in guns

            b. What the Bible is good for

            c. Do we trust God?

ACTIVITIES

1. Role Play. Pair your students off and have them take turns arguing whether Jesus ever lived. If arguing the unbeliever's part is going to challenge your students' maturity too much, you take that part, and have the class argue the Christian side with you.

- Unbelieving side: Your goal is to get your Christian discussion partner away from the Bible and arguing based on reason, science, evidence...anything but depending on God.
- Christian side: Your goal is to keep appealing to God and His Word. Never give up your ultimate authority. You are going to feel a little silly, and that's okay. Just don't make the Eve Mistake, and you'll be fine.

There's actually much more to an apologetic conversation than just the above, so this activity is going to be a little artificial. But the point is to sensitize your students to the issue of ultimate authority, because that's the foundation on which we build the other steps that we can take with an unbeliever.

2. Journal Time. Give your students some time to write in their journals, considering the following:

How did you feel, sticking to the Scriptures in the face of an unbelieving challenge? Did you feel confident? Doubtful? Stupid? Can you imagine yourself doing the same thing with an actual unbeliever? Why or why not? Take some time to pray and reflect on what you've learned in this lesson and how it applies to what you felt.

Lesson 1

EVALUATION

1. What was Adam's Mistake? **Adam rebelled against God to become a god for himself.**

2. What was Eve's Mistake? **Eve got herself into a conversation about God, without including God in it, and then was suckered into a "neutral" stance toward God. From there, she was easily deceived into eating the fruit.**

3. Why is it impossible to be neutral toward God? **Because He made us and everything else. We are born owing Him everything.**

4. Can you use the Bible to win an argument with someone who doesn't believe the Bible? **No. But you can use the Bible to win the person, and that's what's important.**

5. If you use the Bible to prove Christianity, isn't that just circular reasoning? **In a certain way, yes. If you use science to prove atheism, isn't that just circular reasoning? Everyone's ultimate authority is self-justifying.**

When a Christian watches a beautiful sunset, he sees the glory of the God who created it. Not so for the unbeliever.

LESSON 2

Devotional Apologetics: Without Excuse

NOTES TO THE TEACHER

The sunset puzzle
Begin this lesson with the same puzzle as we presented in the last lesson. *A Christian and an atheist sit on a hilltop together watching the sunset. The Christian sees God's glory; the atheist sees nothing but molecules in motion. How is that possible?* In this lesson we want to add a wrinkle to this puzzle. Psalm 19 says that the heavens declare the glory of God. So...do they, or don't they?

The challenge here is to avoid the Eve Mistake; in order to do that we must start with what God says. God says that the heavens declare the glory of God, so they do. God only made one sky, and there are no atheist sunsets. At the same time, we can't avoid noticing that as these two people watch the sunset, only one of them seems to hear the declaration. How do we account for the fact that God writes His glory across the sky, and the atheist somehow manages not to notice? That is the central question of this lesson.

Let's start with what we already know. When Eve set aside what God told her, tried to assume a neutral stance toward God, and then used her God-given senses and reason from that sinful starting point, she came to exactly the wrong conclusion. If, like Eve, the atheist is coming to the wrong conclusions from looking at a sunset, perhaps he is making the same mistake. But if that is the case, then what is the atheist ignoring? What has God shown him at the outset that he is setting aside?

OVERVIEW

Since we have a different ultimate authority than the unbeliever, how can we talk to him? What point of contact do we have? We have the world, and everything in it. God is always and everywhere confronting the unbeliever with the world, which points everyone to God. Once we understand that, we will be able to talk with the unbeliever about the world in a way that points back to God without making the Eve Mistake.

SOURCE MATERIAL

- Psalm 19
- Romans 1:18-32
- Psalm 14 by Sons of Korah (online video)
- Pearcey and Thaxton, *The Soul of Science*

Biblical foundation: Romans 1:18-32
Paul addresses this very question in Romans chapter 1. He begins the book by greeting the Roman church, and talks about how much he has longed to visit them, but he has been unable. Now, finally, he will be able to come and minister to them (as well as be encouraged by them). He is ready, he says, to proclaim the good news among them—he is not ashamed of the good news, because it is God's power to save, revealing God's righteousness. Paul will go on later in the book to talk about what happens when we believe that good news, but he begins by talking about unbelief, the topic that concerns us today.

Devotional Apologetics

> **OBJECTIVES**
>
> **The student will feel...**
>
> - the challenge of finding a point of contact when ultimate authorities conflict.
> - encouraged that we are surrounded by points of contact.
>
> **The student will understand...**
>
> - that God always and everywhere confronts us with Himself in the world.
> - that the whole world is therefore a point of contact.
> - that the unbeliever actually knows God, but suppresses that knowledge.
> - that in order to avoid the Eve Mistake, we don't argue for God's existence; instead we expose the emptiness of unbelief.
>
> **The student will apply this understanding by...**
>
> - examining the biblical Story for examples of how to interact with unbelief.
> - reflecting on Psalm 14.

God's wrath is revealed from heaven against men *who suppress the truth in unrighteousness*. How can Paul say that they suppress the truth? Because the truth about God is clearly visible among them, because God has shown it to them. God made the world to reveal Himself, and ever since creation the truth about Him—His eternal power and Godhead—has been clearly seen, *and people understand it*. So they have no excuse, because even though they did know God, they refused to glorify Him as God and be thankful to Him. The problem is not that they don't *know* God; the problem is that they don't *like* Him.

It's impossible to commit these sins of dishonesty and ingratitude in isolation. These sins have a ripple effect; the thinking of the one who commits them becomes futile, his heart becomes dark, and he descends into madness. Human beings were made to worship, and if they will not worship God, then they will worship something else, something created. It's foolish, but if you're not going to worship God, that's the only other option. Ingratitude has serious cognitive effects—we'll come back to this shortly.

That ingratitude also has physical and moral effects. In response to their rejection, God gives them over to be so taken with lust that both men and women descend into homosexuality, dishonoring their bodies and receiving the consequences of that. Because they "did not *like* to retain God in their knowledge" (Rom 1:28), God gives them over to every sort of sin—and do pay attention to the list in Romans 1:29-31. Envy, disobedience to parents and untrustworthiness are in the list along with the sodomy that's already been discussed. *All these things are downstream consequences of failure to be grateful to God.*

For our discussion of apologetics, there are two particular things we need to draw out of this passage. First, nobody is actually ignorant of God. Nobody. The problem is not that they don't know God is there; it's that they resent Him because they don't want to say thank you. That resentment leads them to suppress the truth, to bury it as deep as they can. Second, suppressing the truth has cognitive consequences: they "became futile in their thoughts, and their foolish hearts were darkened" (Rom 1:21). "Futile" means that their thinking becomes empty and self-defeating. (Remember this when an unbeliever's defense of his unbelief sounds plausible to you. You have God's word telling you that the unbeliever's thinking is self-defeating and foolish—the foolishness is always there. The argument will always defeat itself—you just have to figure out how.)

Even if he is not devoting his life to solving the mysteries of the universe, the unbeliever still has to buy groceries, eat, breathe, see the sunset, etc. He cannot avoid God's world—it's the only world there is. He must live in this world that is designed to tell him the truth about God, without ever once admitting to himself the truth about God. That's a lot of lying to himself, and it affects his ability to think clearly.

Applying Romans 1 to the sunset puzzle
Let's apply these insights from Romans 1 to the sunset problem. The atheist who sits on a hill watching a sunset *has no excuse* for denying God; he can, in fact, see God's glory revealed in the creation. This does not mean that he's consciously aware of it—he suppresses the truth. But he suppresses the truth because deep down, he does not *want* to say thank you, and if he acknowledges God, he'll have to.

Moreover, when we ask him to account for his position, he is going to profess to be wise, but in fact he will say something foolish, something futile and self-defeating. He can't do anything else—once he has given up on telling the truth about God, there's nothing left but foolishness. "There is no wisdom or understanding or counsel against the Lord" (Prov 21:30). The question is, will we be able to spot the foolishness? It's not as easy as it sounds—unbelievers' arguments often sound pretty good at first. We have to begin by trusting God that the foolishness is there and then seek to uncover it.

Application: Arguing for God's existence
For example, suppose the atheist on the hilltop turns to the Christian and says, "Look, you're not denying that we're seeing molecules in motion out there. We agree on that, right?"

"Sure," says the Christian.

"Okay," says the atheist. "So that's all I believe. You believe something beyond that—you think it means there is a God. So prove it to me."

What now?

Do you see the trap? Paul looks at the atheist and says he is inexcusable, but the atheist is acting like you're the one who needs an excuse. *Don't buy it*. Remember, Paul warned us that they will profess to be wise, but become fools. They will adopt a posture of wisdom. Don't be fooled by the posturing. Look for the underlying foolishness and expose it. Don't think that you can do anything as big as proving God to him. If he has looked squarely at a sunset, seen a hummingbird in flight, watched waves crash on the beach, felt the winter wind bite his cheeks—if he has experienced all these things and still does not believe, what proof do you propose to offer him that is better than that? Can you outdo the sunset?

No, we should answer the challenge by following the Bible's examples. One thing the Bible *never* does is argue for God's existence. The biblical stance is that God's existence is self-evident, and only a fool denies it (Ps 14).

So your first response might be something like this: "No, I don't see molecules in motion. I see a sign from the living God that He's right there, and I want to know why you can't read it!"

When we get into making more serious arguments, Christian apologetics has often been suckered by the Eve Mistake. Below, we're going to look at two examples of talking about God based on the world around us. In the first one, the Christian gives in to the Eve Mistake. In the second, he doesn't.

Approach #1: The cosmological argument
Taking this approach, the believer on the hilltop might argue that we are surrounded by a world of cause and effect—every effect has its cause, which must be prior to it and sufficient to account for it. The sunset is one more effect, and as we inquire into its causes, we encounter such things as weather patterns, the refractive index of air and other materials, and so on. So we move from, "Why is the sunset so red?" to the fundamental laws of the universe, and thence to the question of what caused the universe. The only possibility that could be prior to the universe and sufficient to account for it, the apologist will say, is God.

However, the atheist has a couple of responses. The first one is that even if the Christian's argument holds, this is a *very* long way from proving the existence of anything like the God of the Bible. All it does is demonstrate the existence of some powerful and intelligent being (or beings) who set the universe in motion—a being which might just as easily be evil as good, a being who might be entirely unconcerned about us, etc. Of course, the Christian can counter with an assortment of other arguments designed to show the goodness of the supreme being and so on. We'll come back to that in a moment.

The atheist's second objection, though, will be much more telling. "What caused God?" he says. The Christian patiently explains that nothing caused God, that God is the Ultimate Cause of everything that happens. Now at this point the atheist has two options. First, he could argue for an infinite regression of causes, such that there actually is no Ultimate Cause. In response, the Christian will have to argue that an Ultimate Cause is somehow logically necessary—the chain of causality can't keep going back forever; it's actually got to stop somewhere. However, even if the Christian wins that argument, the atheist has another, better card to play: given the necessity for an Ultimate Cause, why shouldn't the universe itself be the Ultimate Cause? The Christian is assuming that the universe itself is an effect that requires a cause—but that was the very thing the Christian was supposed to prove!

Approach #2: Accounting for causality
In this approach, the Christian begins by assuming that the atheist does in fact know God, and despite suppressing that knowledge, gives evidence of knowing God through the way that he lives in God's world. To take this tack, the Christian is not going to make an argument about the world so much as he is going to make an argument about the unbeliever and the nature of his unbelief.

In this strategy, the Christian will address the same principle of causality, but move in an entirely different direction. The question is not "What's the cause of everything?" but "Since we know cause and effect works, how do we account for it?"

Suppose a man wakes up hungry in the middle of the night. He makes his way downstairs, and passing through the living room on the way to the kitchen, he stubs his toe on the leg of the coffee table. He hops around and mutters a quiet curse or two, then limps into the kitchen and gets himself a snack. Passing back through the living room on his way to bed, he stubs his toe on the leg of the coffee table again. Again, he hops around, mutters quiet curses, and then limps back upstairs. A few hours later, he wakes up hungry again. He goes downstairs, and then *very carefully* walks around the coffee table to protect his tender toes.

Why does he avoid stubbing his toes on the coffee table? Because it's going to hurt, of course. How does he know that it's going to hurt? Because it did the last two times. Now here's the question: *how does he know that the third time won't be the thrill of a lifetime?*

This seems like a silly question, but it's not. It seems silly because everybody knows that it's going to hurt. Fair enough—but *why* does everybody know that? Why is it the sort of universe in which something that hurt the first two times is going to hurt the third time? We all know it's true, but *how do we account for it?*

Christians have a ready answer to this question. The universe was made orderly by Yahweh, the God of the Bible, who is orderly Himself. He made the world for humanity and humanity for the world, and so the world is organized in such a way as to be comprehensible to us, if we work at it. Simple.

But how is an unbeliever going to account for it? Suppose the universe is in fact the place of random chance that he thinks—how does he know stubbing his toe will hurt? How does he know gravity will work tomorrow? Because it always has in the past? How does he know that things will work tomorrow like they have in the past? (By the way, this is not a trivial question; philosophers have routinely struggled to account for the uniformity of nature, and David Hume destroyed the unbelieving philosophical basis for understanding it centuries ago. To date, no one has successfully answered him.)

Do you see the difference in approaches? In the first approach, we are trying to prove something to the unbeliever using the principle of causality. In the second approach, we question whether the unbeliever has any right to appeal to causality at all. Of course he knows that causality works, and that's the point. But he can't account for it, can't give any reason why he ought to trust it. In his heart of hearts, he knows causality works *because he knows that God is behind it*—but instead of worshipping God and being thankful, he denies Him. So he ends up with no choice but to believe in causality as a blind leap of faith, while the Christian is able to give account for it.

Example: The possibility of science
Pearcey & Thaxton, *The Soul of Science*, offers a valuable explanation of how a thousand years of Christianity in Europe created unique intellectual and cultural conditions that allowed modern science to arise and flourish. The book argues that modern science could not have arisen in a society that did not have a number of key Christian presuppositions. If you want to dig into the argument in detail, you will find it in the first chapter of the book.

Psalm 14 offers a biblical meditation on atheism. We encourage you to let your students hear the psalm as it was meant to be heard—as a song. Sons of Korah have set it to music, and videos are available online.

Devotional Apologetics

TEACHING OUTLINE

I. Introduction and review
   A. Teacher begins class by leading them in the Lord's Prayer: **"Our Father, who art in heaven, hallowed be Thy name. Thy kingdom come. Thy will be done on earth as it is in heaven. Give us this day our daily bread, and forgive us our trespasses, as we forgive those who trespass against us. And lead us not into temptation, but deliver us from evil. For Thine is the kingdom, and the power, and the glory forever and ever. Amen."**
   B. Today's place on the path: We've learned to stick with God's authority and pay attention to Him. But if we have a different ultimate authority than the unbeliever, then how can we talk to him at all? What possible point of contact can we have?

II. Today's lesson
   A. Introduction: sunsets and Psalm 19
   B. Biblical foundation: Romans 1:18-32
      1. Without excuse
      2. Futile in their thoughts
      3. Romans 1 and the sunset problem
   C. Application: arguing for God's existence
      1. The Bible doesn't
      2. Cosmological argument
      3. An argument about causality and unbelief
   D. Example: the possibility of science

ACTIVITIES

1. Thinking Through the Story. Throughout the biblical Story, there are many encounters between God's people and those who do not believe in Him. Make a list of these encounters and what happens at each one. How do God's people approach those who don't believe in Him? How do the unbelievers respond? What can we learn from these past encounters?

2. Journal Time: Reflecting on Psalm 14. We suggest you have your students listen to a musical version of Psalm 14. Sons of Korah has a nice arrangement available online. After listening to the psalm, give your students the opportunity to reflect on the psalm in their journals.

Lesson 2

EVALUATION

1. What biblical passage gives us an example of how to make a rational proof for God's existence? **Trick question—there isn't one. The Bible never tries to offer a rational proof for God's existence.**

2. According to the Bible, how does anyone know that God is there? **The creation announces His presence, and everyone knows that He is there.**

3. If everyone knows that God is there, then why are there so many atheists? **They suppress the truth.**

4. Why would anyone suppress the truth about God? **Because they don't like Him. They don't want to have to say thank you.**

5. If we don't argue for God's existence based on the world, then what do we do? **We expose the emptiness of unbelief. We argue that the unbeliever is suppressing the truth, based on the world.**

6. How do we expose the emptiness of unbelief when it comes to cause and effect? **We show how as Christians, we have a way of accounting for an orderly, cause and effect universe. We challenge the unbeliever to account for his faith in cause and effect, even though he doesn't believe in God.**

Adam and Eve failed because they forgot what God had said, distorting their reasoning and leading to sin. Everything worth having or knowing is hidden in Christ.

LESSON 3

Devotional Apologetics: Don't Get Robbed!

NOTES TO THE TEACHER

Last lesson, we looked at the futility and self-deception that inevitably follow from the unbeliever's deliberate refusal to glorify and thank God. We saw how Paul tells us that the unbeliever's thinking becomes self-defeating, and in practice he can't fit the truth into his way of looking at the world.

It's actually much worse than that. The other side of the coin is that *if* the unbeliever were consistent with his unbelieving principles, *he couldn't know anything at all*. Every last useful bit of truth would be completely inaccessible to him, the sole property of the Christian. We could demonstrate this by logical inference from Romans 1, but there's no need for a complicated argument. The Bible says this much more directly; and so in this lesson we're going to look at this truth and consider its implications for discussion with an unbeliever.

In Colossians 2, Paul is urging Christians to focus on Christ, and in the process he says that all the treasures of wisdom and knowledge are hidden in Christ. But what does this mean? Well, a treasure is something valuable, something worth having. Biblically, "wisdom" is a generic word for skill. It might be skill in various trades (see Exod 31:3, 35:26, 35:31, 33, 35), the skill to end a war (2 Sam 20:22), or skill to govern well (2 Chr 1:10). At its most basic, "knowledge" is command of the facts. So we might say that "all the treasures of wisdom and knowledge" means "all the skills worth having and all the facts worth knowing."

OVERVIEW

An unbeliever necessarily denies the truth that he knows about God, but in reality he suppresses much more than just his knowledge of God. If the unbeliever is consistent with his unbelieving principles, it turns out that in fact he could know nothing at all. In Colossians 2, Paul teaches us that *all* the treasures of wisdom and knowledge are hidden in Christ. He also tells us that if we forget this truth, we get robbed.

SOURCE MATERIAL

- Colossians 2:1-10
- J. Budziszewski, *What We Can't Not Know*
- Optional: James Nickel, *Mathematics: Is God Silent?*

Paul's claim is that all the skills worth having and all the facts worth knowing are hidden in Christ. Do we believe him? For many of us, this is as hard to believe as last lesson's claim that the unbeliever really does know God, deep down. But as with the last lesson, if we are willing to accept the biblical claim at face value and ask God to give us eyes to see it, then we will find that evidence is everywhere we look.

The alternative—if we do not believe Paul—is to go looking apart from Christ for the wisdom and knowledge that we need to live our daily lives. When we do that, Paul says, we get robbed "through philosophy and empty deceit,

Devotional Apologetics

> **OBJECTIVES**
>
> **The student will feel...**
>
> - initial confusion and consternation over the claim that *all* the treasures of wisdom and knowledge are hidden in Christ.
> - growing confidence that Paul's claim could really be true.
> - concern over getting robbed by failing to believe what God says.
>
> **The student will understand...**
>
> - that the Bible really does say that *all* the treasures of wisdom and knowledge are hidden in Christ.
> - that "treasures of wisdom and knowledge" means skills worth having and facts worth knowing.
> - how to challenge the futility of the unbelieving basis for morality.
> - how to explain the biblical basis for moral living.
> - how to address the problem of evil at a basic level.
>
> **The student will apply this understanding by...**
>
> - practicing challenging an unbeliever's basis for morality.
> - prayerfully considering his own doubts (if any) about all the treasures of wisdom and knowledge being hidden in Christ.

according to the tradition of men [and] according to the basic principles of the world" (Col 2:8). This turns into another form of the Eve Mistake. Instead of engaging God, we search apart from Him for knowledge about how the world works, and we end up thinking of the way the world works as "just there" rather than appointed to work that way by God's decree.

Application: Morality
One good place to look is morality. Everybody has morality in two senses. First of all, Romans 1 has already told us that everyone knows certain moral truths, however much they may claim otherwise. Second, and even more basic, everyone makes moral claims, no matter how twisted. Certain courses of action are right; others are wrong.

In other words, people know, however much they might try to deny it, that a baby in the womb is, in fact, a person, and killing the baby is murder. That's the first point. The second point is that even when they're not willing to admit to knowing certain moral truths, they still make moral claims. So the people who say that abortion is a woman's right will hold that it's wrong to force a pregnant mother to carry her child to term. This is still a moral claim—a deeply backwards one, to be sure, but a moral claim all the same.

That second point is where we are going to spend our time in this lesson: even people who can't agree on what is morally right or wrong will still agree that there is such a thing as moral right and wrong. (Occasionally someone will even deny that—but steal his French fries and see how he reacts.)

As you speak with the unbeliever, you will discover that he wants to claim that certain things are right and others are wrong. Stealing his French fries, for example, is wrong. Hitler killing six million Jews in WWII was wrong. An innocent child dying of leukemia is wrong. In fact, he may even want to lay some of these charges at God's feet: "How can your God let these things happen?"

We'll come back to how to address that question in a little bit. First, though, let's address the question of standards. How can this person who refuses to acknowledge God claim that something is right or wrong? What could it possibly mean that something is right or wrong in a godless world?

As it happens, unbelieving philosophers have struggled with that question and have come up with some answers. Broadly speaking, the answers break down into consequential theories of morality and approval theories of morality. Consequential theories argue that the good action is the one that brings about a good consequence (or can reasonably be expected to bring about a good consequence). Leaving aside the problems involved in trying to predict the consequences of your action, and what constitutes a reasonable prediction, all consequential theories fall prey to one basic problem: in the end, consequential theories just back the problem up a step. If we can decide which actions are good based on whether the consequences are good, then who decides which consequences are good?

Approval theories, on the other hand, hold that actions are good or bad based on the approval of some authority or another, usually society or some elite group. The problem here is—who says we have to follow the judgment of that particular group? Why that particular group and not some other group?

Many unbelievers will try to appeal to society as a whole. So for example, when you ask whether it was wrong for Hitler to kill six million Jews, they want to be able to say yes. You will point out the society Hitler was living in seemed to largely approve of Hitler and his policies. Hitler passed laws; what he did to the Jews was legal according to the laws of the land at the time he did it. Doesn't that make it okay? No, your friend will say, because the society as a whole was much bigger than just Germany. The Western world as a whole condemned what Germany did. Great, so that makes something okay as long as we all agree on it? So, in, say, the year 1700, when the whole Western world agreed that kidnapping and enslaving Africans was okay—it really was okay? And everything that the whole Western world is doing now—is it really all okay, as long as we say it is?

You see the problem? No one wants to say that kidnapping and slavery was okay back in the day, just not now. Everyone wants to be able to say that we are making some mistakes now—but if whatever we approve is okay, then we aren't making any mistakes now, are we?

The biblical answer to morality
God made us to be a creaturely reflection of Himself. We are designed to act according to His character, and we ought not to depart from that design. Moral actions are those that reflect the revealed character of God, and immoral actions are those that do not properly portray the image of God.

An astute student will notice that this is an approval theory—actions that meet with God's approval are moral; those that do not are immoral. So the challenge is, "Who is God, that we should care about His approval?" God Himself has given us the answer: He is the maker, sustainer and owner of everything, including us. And He is the judge, in the end, of how we have lived.

Devotional Apologetics

As Christians, we have a succinct and consistent account for morality. Meanwhile, the unbeliever has none—yet he persists in wanting to make moral judgments. By making moral judgments, he is revealing that he does, in fact, know that God is there.

The problem of evil

The schizophrenia of unbelief is never more apparent than when the unbeliever is challenging a Christian with the problem of evil. "If God is good and all-powerful, then why do all these bad things happen?"

There are a couple of important ways to answer this question, depending on who is asking. A lot of the people who ask this question aren't asking for intellectual reasons. They want to know why their cousin's baby died, or why their spouse got killed in a car accident, or why their life savings got wiped out by identity theft. When it's that kind of question, the answer you give is, "I don't know." Because *you don't*. Then you love the person as best you can.

If it's an intellectual question, you can take a different angle. You can ask, "What bad things?" Get some examples—infants with leukemia, good people getting murdered, the Holocaust, whatever. Then ask, "Why are they bad?"

The unbeliever will look at you like you're crazy. He might say something like, "If you can't figure out why tiny babies dying of cancer is a bad thing, then I feel sorry for you!" Then you get to say this: "I can figure out why that's bad. It's bad because that's not what God designed the world to be. What I can't figure out is, why do *you* think it's bad? If the world is just an accident, and it's not supposed to be any particular way, then what difference does it make? Maybe you don't personally like babies having cancer, but why should anybody care what you think?"

Of course in reality, you know why the unbeliever thinks babies dying of cancer is bad. He thinks it's bad because he is made in the image of God. By questioning him, you're insisting that if he is going to criticize God, he has to account for the standard that he's using—and he can't do it.

What the unbeliever has to do is borrow a standard from us, refuse to admit it, and then turn that standard against God. But once he's done that, he has stepped into the biblical worldview, and within that worldview, there's a clear and compelling answer to his concerns. Babies having cancer *is* bad; we don't deny it. We take the matter to God in prayer and ask for relief, because it is a bad thing. Why does God allow it to happen? We don't know. But we trust that God allows it *for reasons that are perfectly sufficient to Him, even if they are unknown to us*. That is what Scripture teaches us to do—trust God.

Resources

If you want to dig deeper into the subject of universally known moral truths (murder is wrong, etc.), we recommend that you read J. Budziszewski's *What We Can't Not Know*. Budziszewski works through what we know and how we know it. Equally important, he shows how we rationalize our way around what we know in order to suppress the truth and do what we want to do.

It may be too advanced for your students, but many people who can see how morality is obviously rooted in a moral Lawgiver still wonder how it can be that *all* the treasures of wisdom and knowledge are hidden in Christ. How is it, for example, that the fundamental truths of mathematics are hidden in Christ? To dig deeper into this area, we recommend James Nickel's *Mathematics: Is God Silent?*

Lesson 3

TEACHING OUTLINE

I. Introduction and review

   A. Teacher begins class by leading them in the Lord's Prayer: **"Our Father, who art in heaven, hallowed be Thy name. Thy kingdom come. Thy will be done on earth as it is in heaven. Give us this day our daily bread, and forgive us our trespasses, as we forgive those who trespass against us. And lead us not into temptation, but deliver us from evil. For Thine is the kingdom, and the power, and the glory forever and ever. Amen."**

   B. Today's place on the path: We've seen the basic mistakes we can make in understanding the world—the Adam Mistake of rebellion and the Eve Mistake of forgetting to start with God. We've seen how when an unbeliever suppresses the truth that he clearly knows, self-deception and futility inevitably follow, and he can't fit the truth into his way of looking at the world. Today, we look at another crucial implication of the unbeliever's suppression of truth.

II. Today's lesson

   A. Biblical grounding: Colossians 2:1-10

   B. Example: morality

     1. Godless theories of morality

        a. Consequential theories

        b. Approval theories

     2. A biblical answer

     3. Addressing the problem of evil

ACTIVITIES

1. Apologetic Practice. Pair off and take turns pretending to be an unbeliever. Let the believer challenge the unbeliever's basis for any kind of morality, and let the unbeliever defend it the best he can. For a second round, have the unbeliever go on the offensive and attack the believer with the problem of evil, and let the believer defend himself the best he can.

2. Journal Time. How do you feel about the claim that *all* the facts worth knowing and *all* the skills worth having are hidden in Christ? Why do you think Paul says that? Do you think it's true? How could you know if it's true or not? We suggest you let your students journal on these questions for a while, and then discuss it in class. Remind them that God plainly says it and point to the role of the Adam Mistake and the Eve Mistake in our reactions to what seems an outlandish claim.

Lesson 3

EVALUATION

1. What does Colossians 2 say is hidden in Christ? **All the treasures of wisdom and knowledge**

2. What is a "treasure of wisdom?" Give three examples. **A treasure of wisdom is a skill worth having. Examples can be extremely varied, from "how to be a good friend" to "weaving a basket" to "helping a suicidal person."**

3. What is a "treasure of knowledge?" Give three examples. **A treasure of knowledge is a fact worth knowing. Examples can be extremely varied, from "murder is wrong" to "2+2=4" to "God loves me."**

4. What is the biblical basis for morality? **God made the entire world and gives it purpose. He designed us to be images of Him, so good actions are those which image God's character well, and bad actions are those which image God's character poorly.**

5. Give two of the unbelieving theories for the basis of morality. **Approval theories (good actions are those approved by a certain authority) and consequential theories (good actions are those that bring good consequences).**

6. Why do the unbelieving theories for morality fail? **Approval theories fail because they can't establish the legitimacy of the authority. Consequential theories fail because they have no way of defining a good consequence.**

The rebels had to build the tower of Babel out of God's earth; they couldn't make their own. Everything people build to avoid dealing with God is built with what God gave them, and founded in the world He made.

LESSON 4

Devotional Apologetics: Answer a Fool

NOTES TO THE TEACHER

The preceding three lessons have been far more about understanding what's really going on in the clash between belief and unbelief than they have been about how to talk to an unbeliever in an apologetic encounter. We have used some sample discussions and arguments to illustrate various points, but that's it. This lesson, however, focuses on the biblical standards for interaction with unbelievers in an apologetic conversation.

We have already discussed how the Scriptures describe the unbeliever as a fool. This is not saying that they're stupid, for unbelievers can be incredibly smart. But by refusing to acknowledge and thank God, unbelievers become foolish: dark in their hearts and futile and self-deceived in their thinking. What does Scripture tell us about speaking with such people?

One of the really important biblical passages is Proverbs 26:4-5, and it gives us two key standards to go by. "Do not answer a fool according to his folly, lest you also be like him. Answer a fool according to his folly, lest he be wise in his own eyes." The apparent contradiction is not there by accident; it highlights the difficulty inherent in trying to speak to a fool.

The first standard is not to answer a fool in such a way that we descend to his level. The obvious application is that if the person is abusive or insulting, we do not return their abuse and insults. A more subtle, but equally important application, is not to accept the unbeliever's invitation to join him in the Eve Mistake of pretended neutrality. We do not argue based on

OVERVIEW

It's one thing to know that the unbeliever's position is self-defeating, but it's another thing entirely to find the weaknesses and expose them so that the unbeliever can see the weaknesses—and do all that without sinking to the unbeliever's level at the same time. In this lesson, we learn the biblical standards for interacting with unbelief and observe some examples of people who do it well.

SOURCE MATERIAL

- Proverbs 26:4-5
- *Collision* DVD (documentary on the debates between Doug Wilson and Christopher Hitchens)
- The Bahnsen/Stein debate (available from Covenant Media Foundation and in various places online)

some other ultimate authority than the Word of God, which we know to be true.

We need to underscore just how important it is that we not forsake our ultimate authority. We have a relationship with the Living God. We should never—not for a moment, not "for the sake of argument," *never*—pretend that we don't. For you as a Christian to pretend that you don't know God exists in order to "meet the unbeliever where he is" is like a husband pretending he's single in order to "meet the single girls where they're at." Don't do it.

Devotional Apologetics

OBJECTIVES

The student will feel...

- daunted by the challenge of letting the unbeliever feel the foolishness of his position without sinking to his level.
- encouraged that God is the one who makes it possible to meet the challenge.

The student will understand...

- that "do not answer a fool according to his folly" means not to sink to his level.
- that "answer a fool according to his folly" means not to let him be wise in his own eyes—help him see the foolishness of his position.
- that unbelieving arguments often initially seem plausible, but the foolishness is always there.

The student will apply this understanding by...

- observing how Greg Bahnsen exposes the foolishness of the unbelieving position in his debate.
- observing how Doug Wilson is able to do the same, but be friendly at the same time.

Never fail to acknowledge that God is present. The last thing Jesus said to us was "Lo, I am with you always" (Matt 28:20). He is right here. Believe it, live it, and always portray that to the unbelievers in your life.

The second standard is to answer the unbeliever's folly in such a way that it prevents him from being wise in his own eyes. Paul says "professing to be wise, they became fools" (Rom 1:22), and it is our job to find the foolishness and show it to them. If the unbeliever leaves the discussion thinking that his skepticism about Yahweh is a prudent, wise thing, then we have not met this standard.

That means proving that the unbeliever is being unreasonable or illogical is not nearly enough. Remember our biblical grounding here—he *is* being unreasonable, and we already know it. If you walk away from the conversation thinking, "Well, I proved that he was being illogical, but he just won't see it," you have not met the standard. *Him seeing it is the standard*.

He will, of course, be absolutely opposed to seeing his own foolishness, and he will use all his intelligence to oppose you as you try to show it to him. And unless the Spirit opens his eyes, he will be successful—he will leave the conversation as foolish as he came, still thinking that he's wise, despite your best efforts.

Your job is to be the Spirit's vessel, to ask the Spirit to give you wisdom to know how best to talk with this person. Trust what God has said—the foolishness is there, whether you can see it or not. Ask the Spirit to give you the eyes to see the foolishness for what it is and guide you in exposing it so your friend can't miss it, so he can't un-see it.

You will not always be successful, and that's okay. Your job is to be a faithful servant. It is the Spirit's job to open your friend's eyes.

The trouble with trying to meet the Proverbs 26 standard for apologetic discussion is that it's *really hard*. It can be very difficult for us to see where the foolishness resides in the unbeliever's argument, and even when we can see it, explaining it so the unbeliever sees it can be even harder. Let's talk about these two problems.

Initially, unbelieving arguments often look alarmingly plausible. You should admit this to your students up front. Let them know that it's okay if their first impression of the opposing argument is "<gulp> Looks like he's got a point." We've all been there, and it's okay. That moment is an opportunity to trust God. Trust that there is folly in there. You don't even have to look for it yet—the first job is to be winning and kind to the unbeliever in front of you.

When it looks hopeless, smile at the unbeliever. Don't get cranky. Say, "You know, nobody's ever said it to me quite like that before. Let me make sure I understand what you're saying." Then ask questions to make sure you understand the unbeliever's argument clearly. Don't try to argue at this point, just be sure you understand. The arguing can happen later. Once you're confident you understand the argument, say, "I'm not sure what I think of that right this minute. Let me think about it for a little while, and I'll get back to you."

Take the argument home and lay it out before the Lord. Don't immediately start picking at it, looking for logical fallacies—that comes later. First pray. Put it before God, and ask Him to show you the foolishness in the argument. Wait for an answer. See what God will say to you. If nothing occurs to you in the moment, go ahead and start studying the argument. Look for fallacies; do your research; ask your pastor or other experienced people for help.

Using the Collision DVD
We recommend you use the *Collision* DVD at this point in the unit. It furnishes a straightforward example of how to talk with an unbeliever on the basis of the four key points of the Support Structure. The next three lessons will be devoted to a deeper understanding of how to communicate Christianity winsomely, but if these first four lesson were all you had, you could do what Wilson does in this set of debates.

Tell the students to pay particular attention to Wilson's arguments and strategy. Things to notice:

"By what standard?" is the constant drumbeat of Wilson's argument. Over and over, in every arena, he asks the same question.

In moral argument, Wilson challenges the possibility of an atheist standard. When they ask how a good God could allow the Holocaust, he asks how they can condemn the Holocaust as evil, if it's just bags of protoplasm killing each other.

Also be sure your students don't miss the larger elements of strategy beyond Wilson's arguments:

Wilson is unfailingly polite and good-humored. He is never cranky, never angry. He is always *relaxed*.

Wilson cultivates a genuine friendship with Hitchens. They share common interests, eat together, laugh together.

The Bahnsen/Stein debate
You will have to use your judgment on whether you will play the Bahnsen/Stein debate for your students, or perhaps have them listen to it for homework, or even read it aloud (a transcript is available online). We have found it very helpful for illustrating the contrast between arguing in traditional, incremental fashion for the existence of God as over against the kind of approach we are teaching here. This debate is particularly useful because Dr. Stein came prepared to argue against the incremental approach, but Bahnsen never used it, instead doing something else entirely.

Devotional Apologetics

TEACHING OUTLINE

I. Introduction and review

  A. Teacher begins class by leading them in the Lord's Prayer: **"Our Father, who art in heaven, hallowed be Thy name. Thy kingdom come. Thy will be done on earth as it is in heaven. Give us this day our daily bread, and forgive us our trespasses, as we forgive those who trespass against us. And lead us not into temptation, but deliver us from evil. For Thine is the kingdom, and the power, and the glory forever and ever. Amen."**

  B. Today's place on the path: Knowing what God has shown us about what's happening in the unbeliever's heart, we can now see the bankruptcy of unbelief. What are the biblical standards that govern how we talk with an unbeliever?

II. Today's lesson

  A. The biblical standard (Prov 26:4-5)

   1. Don't sink to the fool's level.

   2. Don't let him be wise in his own eyes.

  B. Viewing *Collision*

  C. Reading the Bahnsen-Stein debate

ACTIVITIES

1. *Collision*. Watch *Collision*. You may want to pause the DVD throughout to discuss certain arguments and strategies that Wilson and Hitchens used. After the movie, discuss the following questions with your students.

- Describe Doug Wilson's demeanor and attitude throughout the movie. What was his relationship with Christopher Hitchens like?
- What question did Wilson ask over and over?
- Where did you see foolishness in Hitchens' presentation? **Various answers are possible. One example would be the way that Hitchens constantly used morally loaded words (e.g., "Christianity is a wicked cult") without being able to explain what "wicked" might mean in a chance universe.**

2. Bahnsen-Stein Debate. Locate the transcripts of the Bahnsen-Stein debate online. Have your class read the debate out loud, rotating readers frequently. We suggest splitting the classroom in half and drawing Bahnsen readers from one side and Stein readers from the other, just to help keep straight who is speaking (particularly important in the cross-examination). After (and perhaps at strategic intervals during) the debate, pause to discuss the arguments. You may wish to use some of the following questions to spur discussion.

Lesson 4

- What is Bahnsen's core argument? What is Stein's?
- Do you think Bahnsen's argument works? What about Stein's?
- Why do you think Bahnsen didn't argue along the lines Stein was expecting?
- Did Stein respond to Bahnsen's argument?
- Do you think it was possible for Stein to respond to Bahnsen's argument? How?
- Where did you see foolishness in Stein's argumentation? **Various answers are possible. Start with the fact that he never actually addressed Bahnsen's position and proceed from there.**

EVALUATION

1. What is the biblical standard for interacting with a fool? **Don't descend to his level, but do expose his foolishness so he can see it.**

2. What does "answer a fool according to his folly" mean? **It means to expose his foolishness, so he won't leave the conversation wise in his own eyes.**

3. What does "do not answer a fool according to his folly" mean? **It means do not sink to his level.**

4. Why are we referring to the unbeliever as a fool? Isn't that rude? **The Bible says, "The fool has said in his heart, 'There is no God'" (Ps 14:1). So he is a fool by biblical definition.**

5. Should we call the unbeliever a fool when we're talking to him? **Probably not. But you need to know, for yourself, that his position is foolish.**

When Adam and Eve sinned, they broke the world and were sent out from the garden. But God sent His Son to bring hope and healing. We are called to participate in His victory in this broken world by loving others.

LESSON 5

Devotional Apologetics: Loving the Different

NOTES TO THE TEACHER

This lesson is the turning point in the unit. Up until now, we have focused on why the unbelieving point of view is wrong and how we can think about it properly. We have looked at some very basic ways to expose the indefensible foolishness of unbelief for what it is, and that approach has its place.

Why the Support Structure doesn't win people
But let's face it, it's a pretty minimal place, if we're talking about dealing with unbelievers. Think about it—in which of your relationships with friends, spouse, or family members is it helpful to tell people all the reasons why you're right and they're wrong? When is that ever a helpful thing to do? Not that often, right?

Exactly.

The real purpose of the four Support Structure lessons is to ground you, as a believer, in your faith. It is to help you understand unbelief so you can handle the assaults on your faith that come from daily interaction with unbelievers. It is to help your students not lose their faith. And every once in a while, yeah, it will come in handy when you need to bloody an unbeliever's nose just to get him to stop assaulting you and have a civil conversation.

But how do people usually come to the faith? It's very rare that someone comes to Christ because he lost an argument. What brings people is not arguments and counter-arguments, but a positive presentation of the truth. As Christians,

OVERVIEW

God made a world where we have the privilege to be His self-portrait by living loving lives. When we love each other, and especially when we love people who are unlovely or who hate us, we are the image of God. You may never argue an unbeliever into feeling the foolishness of his unbelief, but any Christian can love, and love shows up the foolishness of unbelief as nothing else can.

SOURCE MATERIAL

- Genesis 1-2
- John 14-17
- 1 John

we do that by living and telling the true Story of the world. As St. Gregory Palamas said, "For every argument there is a counter-argument, but who can argue against life?"

Even in Acts 17, when Paul is talking to the philosophers in Athens, He tells the Story (albeit in a highly compressed way). Even in the compressed way he tells the Story, Paul raises key points that undergird loving one another. God made every nation of men from one blood, he says to the very racist Greeks.

We too ought to tell the Story, and the Story is like a diamond—there are many different facets to look at, and you can't see them all at once. Every telling of the Story is turning the diamond

Devotional Apologetics

OBJECTIVES

The student will feel...

- reluctant to embrace the challenge of loving other people deeply and well. (Love is costly, and we are all reluctant when we see the real cost—if your students aren't a little reluctant, they don't really understand.)
- empowered and encouraged that even if he can't argue well, he can love people into the kingdom of God.

The student will understand...

- that argument is helpful sometimes, but it doesn't usually win people to Christ.
- that loving people really does win people to Christ.
- that the Story is a love story and can be told that way.
- how to tell the Story as the story of God's love for humanity.

The student will apply this understanding by...

- reading the Upper Room Discourse every day for a week, and noticing its effect on him.
- seeking out three concrete ways to image God's love in the way that he lives.

a particular way, highlighting certain facets over others. Generally speaking, every telling of the Story will also be cutting against some particular failure of the pagan worldview—this is the way that our storytelling fulfills Proverbs 26. By showing how the Christian Story fulfills particular human needs, aspirations and longings, we demonstrate the wisdom of God's truth. By showing how this Story, and its associated way of living, is more fulfilling than the pagan alternatives, we expose the foolishness of unbelief—and we can often do this without ever having to directly say anything about the pagan view. When you offer a real pie to a child playing with a mud pie, you usually don't need to say anything bad about the mud pie—the advantages of the real one are obvious enough.

The Trinitarian love story

This telling of the Story begins with God, who is Love. It is possible for Him to be Love because God is not a solitary being; He is three in one. (Do not underestimate the importance of this point. Religions that start with solitary/unitarian monotheism have a difficult time understanding God's love. Islam is a prime example.) Within the Triune Godhead, love is already being expressed as the Father loves the Son and Spirit, the Son loves the Father and Spirit, and the Spirit loves the Son and the Father. There is perfect love, equality and unity, but there is also distinction—the Father is not the Son is not the Spirit. Each of the three persons is different from the other two.

This infinite, loving community chose to make a representation, an image of itself. A self-portrait, if you like. So God created light and separated it from darkness, separated the waters above from the waters below, and so on. From the very first day of creation, God established that different elements work harmoniously together; as Psalm 19 and Romans 1 say, the whole creation reflects His glory. But within the creation self-portrait, there is one special part, one part that, all by itself, is the image of God. On the sixth day, God created a man. It was the only time in the whole creation process that He said something was not good. It's as if the Triune God set out to make a self-portrait, made a solitary person, then looked in the mirror and said, "No, that's not right"—and then made woman. He looked at the two together and said, "Now that's very good."

God brought the woman to the man and gave them to each other. Adam recognized her for what she was—"This is now bone of my bone, and flesh of my flesh" (Gen 2:23). She was part of him—there was an essential unity between them. And yet, she was not him. In this picture, the first marriage, we have the love of the Trinity acted out—love for the other, for a different person.

So far so good, but of course then we blew it. Adam rebelled, Eve was deceived, and sin and death entered the world. In other words, we broke the world, and we broke it so badly we couldn't possibly fix it. Nowhere is that brokenness more visible than in marriage, the very place that is supposed to be the greatest portrait of the Triune God. As any married person can attest, virtually every problem in marriage is traceable to our own selfishness and the difficulty of loving a person who is genuinely *other* than yourself.

But God still loves His creation, and He still loves us. Like a patient parent who pays for the car repairs his teenage son can't possibly afford, God doesn't insist that we fix everything ourselves. Instead, He took the cost of our sin into Himself. Jesus came. He entered into the broken world as a man, lived in it, and drew into Himself every evil in the whole creation. Holding them all, He died, bearing our griefs and carrying our sorrows into the grave with Him—and then He rose to new life, leaving sin and death broken in the grave.

At that moment, God could have banished all the evil and darkness from the world, but He didn't, *because He wants us to participate in the victory*. He has already won the victory—all the costs are already paid, all the enemies defeated. But now, loving Father that He is, He sends His children out into the world—"All this belongs to Me now. Go and get it."

This is where we are now, and we look forward to the future. Evil is defeated *now*, but one day it will be quarantined, and humanity grown up in Christ will lovingly steward a recreated earth. All impediments to our love for one another and for God's creation will finally be removed, and we will finally love the way God loves—what we were always meant to do.

In the meantime, we live out this love story by loving those who are different, who are unlovely, even those who hate us. As Paul said to the Athenian philosophers, God made from one blood every nation of men—every human being is flesh of my flesh and bone of my bone. We are all sons of Adam and daughters of Eve, and therefore we are united. But boy, are we different!

When I love someone who is not me, someone who is other than me, I am mirroring the love of the Father for the Son and the Spirit, the love of the Son for the Father and the Spirit, the love of the Spirit for the Son and the Father. When I love someone who is unlovely, who doesn't deserve it, perhaps even someone who hates me, I am mirroring the love of God for me and for all humanity. When I love another person, I am being the image of God to that person. If I do my job well, that person will begin to believe that God might love him—because he sees that love in me.

Real Christian witness is always lip and life, and the two must agree as one. Telling the Story is essential; if you just live and never talk, then people just think you're a nice person. God didn't call you to be a nice person; He called you to be an ambassador of His kingdom, and that means you have to speak for Him. But if what you say about Him contradicts the way you live, no one will believe you. Live the Story and tell the Story, and the people you meet will come to know Jesus for themselves.

Reading the Upper Room Discourse
Before Jesus went out to the garden to pray and be arrested, He had one last talk with His disciples. John is the only gospel that records that talk in detail. This was Jesus doing His best to prepare His disciples for living in the world after He had gone back to heaven, and He spent a lot of time teaching about love. Read it often.

Reading 1 John
The book of 1 John is the bane of many a seminary student. It's a common book to study in Greek classes, because John's Greek grammar and vocabulary are so simple, a four-year-old could understand them. But what does it mean? John often seems to speak in riddles, and to students attempting to construct a systematic theology, 1 John is a very difficult book.

Don't read 1 John like a systematic theology or raw material for one. John is speaking as a spiritual father to his little children. Read it that way—as a Dad sitting around the table with his kids after dinner, talking. Meditating on what it's like to live out God's love in real life, what it's like to love God and other people well.

Lesson 5

TEACHING OUTLINE

I. Introduction and review

   A. Teacher begins class by leading them in the Lord's Prayer: **"Our Father, who art in heaven, hallowed be Thy name. Thy kingdom come. Thy will be done on earth as it is in heaven. Give us this day our daily bread, and forgive us our trespasses, as we forgive those who trespass against us. And lead us not into temptation, but deliver us from evil. For Thine is the kingdom, and the power, and the glory forever and ever. Amen."**

   B. Today's place on the path: We have built a solid foundation for understanding what is happening in an unbeliever's heart, and we can use that foundation to win arguments. But the goal was always to win the person, not the argument. How can we best do that?

II. Today's lesson

   A. What the Support Structure lessons were good for

      1. A foundation for yourself

      2. A window into the unbeliever's heart

      3. Occasionally, for arguing well enough to win some respect

   B. What the Support Structure lessons are not good for: winning people

      1. When does it help a relationship to say, "Here are all the reasons I'm right and you're wrong"?

      2. What does help a relationship? Love.

   C. The Trinitarian love story

      1. Imaging intra-Trinitarian love

         a. In the beginning was the Triune God.

         b. Humanity is an image of the Trinity.

         c. Loving the other shows an image of God.

      2. Imaging God's love for us

         a. Loving the unlovely

         b. Loving our enemies and those who hate us

   D. Telling the Trinitarian love story

   E. Living the Trinitarian love story

Devotional Apologetics

ACTIVITIES

1. Telling the Story. The teacher's notes tell the Story as a love story, but use only a few episodes in the Story—creation, the cross, and the new earth. Perhaps using the visual review from the preceding two years, challenge your students to tell the Story a little longer, including more episodes along the way, but still tell it as a love story.

2. Journal Time: A Week in the Upper Room. Challenge your students to read the Upper Room Discourse (John 14-17) every day for a week. Each day, have them make a note of one thing from the discourse that caught their attention. At the end of the week, have them look back over the course of the week and consider whether their time in the upper room changed their behavior in any way. Close out the activity by challenging them to continue the practice for several weeks and see what happens.

3. Loving in Deed and in Truth. "My little children, let us not love in word and in tongue, but in deed and in truth" (1 John 3:18). Have your students list three concrete ways they can image the love of God by doing something definite. Each item should have a definite time boundary—today, tomorrow, this weekend—but at least one should be something they can do today. Check back with them tomorrow to see if they did it. Check back next week to see about the other two. You can't make your students live loving lives, but you can show them a clear path toward living more lovingly and challenge them to take it. See what God will do.

Lesson 5

EVALUATION

1. Can you think of anyone who was ever argued into becoming a Christian? **Most people can't. Josh McDowell and Lew Wallace are famous examples of people who were essentially converted by argument, but these situations are rare. Use this question to underscore how rare it is.**

2. How do you think most people become Christians? **Use this question as a diagnostic tool—find out what your students think. Then challenge them to go to church and do a little survey to find out if their opinion is accurate.**

3. In the Upper Room Discourse, what does Jesus say will convert the world? What do you think it will take for that to happen? **The world will know that the Father sent Jesus when His followers are unified (see John 17:20-23). We will have to learn to love each other if we are ever going to be one.**

4. Other than the ways mentioned already in the lesson, name three episodes in the Story that you could use to talk about how much God loves humanity. **Various answers are possible. For example, how God took care of Elijah when he ran away from Jezebel (1 Kgs 19), how God cared for Nineveh even when His prophet hated them and wanted them to die (Jonah), how Jesus sent His disciples out into the world to tell them the good news that we are all freed from sin (Mark 1:14-15, 16:15).**

5. Name three examples of ways that you can live a more loving life. Be specific. **Various answers are possible, but don't settle for generic answers like "be nicer to my brother." *How?***

Violence entered the world very early—the first son of Adam and Eve killed the second. But, we have matured, and in places around the world where Christianity has had a long-term impact, violence is quite uncommon.

LESSON 6

Devotional Apologetics: Growing to Maturity

NOTES TO THE TEACHER

This lesson tells the same Story as the preceding lesson—there is only one Story. All we're doing here is changing the emphasis, turning the diamond over in our hands so we can see a different facet. In this telling of the Story, the primary focus is on humanity growing into maturity.

We suggest you start telling this Story in the present. We tend to think of our world as a very messed-up place, but in reality things are much better than they used to be in a number of ways. Because things change slowly, however, it's hard to see.

So start with today. What are the real problems in society today? Problems with violence, the environment, breakdown of the family through divorce, a broken healthcare system, unemployment, poverty, homelessness, world hunger...brainstorm with the class and make a big long list. It will be helpful if you can nudge them to get violence on the list a few times.

Tell the students to hold that thought, and then begin to talk with them about the Story in terms of our present problem with violence.

Humanity outgrows violence
The Story begins the same way: God made the world and placed humanity in the garden of Eden, whereupon we broke the world and in the process broke ourselves, becoming sinners

OVERVIEW

Many unbelievers long to see the day that humanity grows up enough to make wise decisions. Different people have different issues that they care about—war, hunger, poverty, business, the environment, family life and so on—but most people care about something and believe that we're messing it up badly. Christianity tells an optimistic story of the world, a story in which humanity really does grow up into maturity, and the world is saved through Jesus Christ.

SOURCE MATERIAL

- Matthew 13:33
- Psalm 2
- Acts 4:23-31
- Revelation 20-21
- *He Shall Crush His Head, Part 2*, Lesson 6.2
- Rodney Stark, *The Rise of Christianity*
- Ramsay MacMullen, *Christianizing the Roman Empire: A.D. 100-400*

by nature as well as by choice. As we look at the world on the nightly news, none of what we see should surprise us—we are sinners, and the world is filled with the consequences of our sin. But that's not the whole Story.

Things got bad very quickly. The first murder was in the second generation. From there,

Devotional Apologetics

OBJECTIVES

The student will feel...

- gratitude that social problems get solved through the slow influence of the gospel.
- perhaps surprise that he has not heard history described in this positive way before.
- elation that Jesus wins in the end, and all the problems go away.

The student will understand...

- that the gospel, operating in society over time, produces real progress.
- that a lot can still be wrong with a society even if it does have the gospel.
- that according to the biblical Story, humanity will eventually grow up and be delivered entirely from all our sins.
- that in the end, Jesus wins.

The student will apply this understanding by...

- naming problems in our world today, committing them to God and thanking Him that in the end, He will resolve them all.
- taking the time to consider whether he really believes that God can resolve all problems, and bringing the problems he has doubts about before God in prayer.

Cain's progeny—cultured, city-building, and murderous—spread over the world. They were at the cutting edge of technology and cultural development, a tribe of Hannibal Lecters, until the whole earth was covered with violence. We think it's bad now. It's not, especially where we live.

We have a school shooting, and the day after, children go to school, and parents all over the country take their kids to the playground (mostly) without fear. We hear on the morning news that a local gas station was robbed—but we go to the gas station on the way to work without a second thought. We do these things because we know in our bones that violence in our society is *rare*, and we're right.

In the pre-Christian corners of the world *right now* there are places where violence is accepted at levels that would be unthinkable for us. Rich Bledsoe, a chaplain in Boulder, CO, relates that when he was teaching at a seminary in India, he told his class how in America, a man who beats his wife can be arrested and go to jail. The class erupted in laughter—they couldn't believe that Americans would be so *stupid*. To them (even to the women), a man smacking his wife around was just normal, everyday married life—and remember, this was a *seminary* class, filled with pastors and their wives.

Sociologist Jared Diamond tells of traveling in New Guinea and being puzzled by the behavior of his native guides. When they met a fellow traveler on the jungle trails, they would sit down and have a lengthy conversation, exchanging family history and genealogy. When he finally asked about it, they explained that someone who was completely unrelated couldn't be trusted not to follow them and kill them in their sleep—so they would have to go ahead and kill him on the spot. That kind of fighting is (obviously) dangerous, so they would sit for several hours if necessary, exchanging information, hoping to find a kinship link that would give them a reason not to kill each other. (For Christians who remember the true Story of the world, the answer is obvious—we're all related as children of Adam through Noah, and that's kinship enough. But in many places in the world, the Story has been forgotten.)

It was even worse in the world that Jesus came into. Even during the period of relative peace brought by Roman rule, bandits along the road were common—so common that Jesus used the banditry along the Jerusalem-Jericho road as the setting for the famous parable of the good Samaritan. That wasn't some imagined scenario; it happened all the time.

Worse than that, in the Roman world, violence was often used as entertainment. Some people complain about the violence in, say, football—but the Romans would flock to see gladiators *kill* each other, or fight wild animals to the death. Tiberius Caesar would have prisoners brought before him and tortured for his amusement while he ate his supper. Can you imagine a world in which someone like that is considered fit for leadership?

We are different from the ancient world and different from the pre-Christian world today. This is not because Americans (or moderns) are somehow naturally better than people in other times and places; it is because the gospel of Jesus Christ has been sinking into our (European) culture for more than 1,500 years. We undoubtedly have a long way to go, but we have also come a very long way—and we should be thankful.

As your students grasp the point, lead them in a prayer of thanksgiving for the work that the gospel has done in the last 2,000 years.

You can do this same kind of meditation with many of the other problems of contemporary society, not only with violence.

Healing the family
Consider the breakdown of the family. We look at what the divorce rate was in, say, 1950, and then look at it today, and we feel like the family is collapsing. We're not wrong about that, but we could benefit from the perspective of the whole Story. God created marriage and family, and He meant it to be one man and one woman united by Him for life. God's plan for the family very quickly degenerated—Cain's descendant Lamech had two wives already, and *that* problem didn't get fixed for a very long time. Jacob had two wives and two concubines, and nobody thought anything of it, even though we can clearly see the relational destruction that happened in his family because of it. David had multiple wives, and he was a servant of God (and again, the tension between children of different mothers escalated to rape and murder). On the question of divorce, though, Jesus reached back to the original intention of creation, and following His lead, the Church made "husband of one wife" (1 Tim 3:2) a requirement for being an elder or a deacon. Even then, it took nearly 800 years to finally get polygamy out of Christian Europe. Polygamy persists in the Arab/Muslim world today, and it's still very common in Africa. But it's a crime in America and Europe. Why? Because the gospel has penetrated our culture very deeply.

Growing up from poverty
Consider poverty. Even in relatively affluent cities like Los Angeles, New York or Denver, there are homeless people living on the street in grinding poverty. It's very difficult—but the lowest of

the low in an American city can stagger into a hospital and get emergency care. There are food banks and rescue missions and homeless shelters, and anyone who wants help can get quite a bit. Why? That's certainly not the case in, say, Mumbai. Nor was it the case in the world that Jesus came into. Notice the circumstances in the parable of the good Samaritan: there were no public institutions to help the man who was beaten and robbed. There was no way to call 911. A private individual rescued him and paid personally for his care. That's the way it was. But no more—and while hospitals began as a notably Christian effort, the gospel has penetrated us so deeply that we now have entirely secular institutions. It's just common sense to us now that we have to take care of these people. But why? Through most of human history, we just stepped over their broken bodies and kept walking (when we didn't regard them as human playthings to be raped, tortured and murdered for our amusement).

Think about poverty from another angle: the richest king of ancient times could do very little to escape the heat of the summer. Maybe he had a basement he could retreat into or a slave with a big fan or something. In America, people who live well below the "poverty line" just turn on the air conditioner. That same king could only eat what was in season, perhaps what could be transported to him by boat or wagon. Today, any poor person with a relatively small amount of money can go to the grocery store and buy grapes and oranges from halfway around the world, in any season. We have had rugs in human history for a long, long time, but in order to clean a rug, you had to take it outside, hang it up, and beat it with a stick. It's a very labor intensive process. (Look online for video of someone using a rug-beater to get a sense of how hard it was to clean the old-fashioned way.) Now, you just run a vacuum cleaner over it, which is a lot easier—and many other cleaning tasks have gotten similarly easier. If you wanted to hear good music skillfully played 100 years ago, you had to go to a city and hear skilled musicians play live, which was very expensive. Today, poor people have CDs and digital music files, and they can hear the best of the best music anytime they want. I (Tim) personally know homeless people with iTunes accounts. All this technology is built on the back of science—iTunes, vacuum cleaners and air conditioners all require electricity, which leads us back to the Leyden jar, which depended on Otto von Guericke's early generator, which in turn relied on William Gilbert's research, published in 1600. The whole thing arose from Western science, which in turn rests on Christianity (see Pearcey and Thaxton, *The Soul of Science*).

Falls, failures and the power of knowing the ending
Now, the above discourse is not to suggest that there are never setbacks. Along the way, there are fits and starts, and whole civilizations rise and fall. Rome fell; Byzantium fell; the Holy Roman Empire fell; the British Empire fell. The Black Death emptied whole villages, as did world wars. But you cannot read Acts and come out thinking that somehow the Church is going to fail in the long term. The kingdom of God is like leaven—once it's in there, it keeps growing, invisibly, until everything is leavened. Christ is building His Church, and the gates of Hades will not prevail against it. The growth of Christ's Church is good for the world, and if we care to look, we can see that there is a positive trend to history.

Knowing that God's kingdom is advancing, we have a spiritually important choice when we come to a setback: we can resent the setbacks and complain, or we can look for the growth of the kingdom of God and be thankful. Psalm 2 teaches us what to do: when the kings of the earth plot to cast off God's rule, He laughs at them. We should laugh with Him. When you read about the next scheme to keep God out of schools, or the marketplace, or any part of the public square, you can think the sky is falling or you can think it's funny. Think it's funny—God does. (And pray like the apostles did in Acts 4:23-31—see the Notes to the Teacher in *He Shall Crush His Head, Part 2*, Lesson 6.2 for more discussion on the relation of these two passages.)

We also should not stop at our point in the Story. We have the future before us, and while none of us knows what will happen tomorrow, we certainly do know how the Story ends. Jesus wins. The human race is delivered by the power of the risen Christ, and the Church grows up in all things into Christ, her head. Evil is quarantined, and in the recreated, curse-free earth, the consequences of the fall are done away with forever. We live in harmony with God and with one another, finally, forever.

Sharing with an unbeliever
Because you know that the Story ends happily, you can have hope when things are bad. Because you know that God is bigger than all our problems, and He will resolve them, you never have to be afraid to take a problem to Him in prayer. You can share the Story (told this way) with an unbeliever, but that's not usually how this approach to evangelism starts.

This approach starts when you realize that there's a problem that's bothering your unbelieving friend. You listen to him talk and perhaps ask him what it is about this particular problem that really bothers him. Hear him out. Then you say something like, "Wow, I can see that this really troubles you. I don't know what you believe about God, but I believe that He wants us to talk to Him about this. Would you mind if I prayed for just a second?"

Then pray. Lay the problem before God. Tell Him you know He's got it, because you've read the end of the Story. Ask Him to do something about the problem. Ask Him to tell you and your friend anything that He wants you to know about the problem, and what you're supposed to do about it, if anything. Listen, and see if He says something to you or your friend.

This is kinda weird, right? Peter tells us to always be ready to give an answer for the hope that is in us. How do you expect that to happen if nobody ever sees you having hope? You are a *Christian*! You have every reason to have hope. If someone sees your unreasonable hope, perhaps then you will have a chance to tell the Story in the way we tell it in this lesson. Share your hope, so that you will have an opportunity to share your faith.

Resources
The two books listed in the resources section, *The Rise of Christianity* by Rodney Stark and *Christianizing the Roman Empire: A.D. 100-400* by Ramsay MacMullen, will help you to get a better grasp of what the world was like when Jesus came into it.

Devotional Apologetics

TEACHING OUTLINE

I. Introduction and review

    A. Teacher begins class by leading them in the Lord's Prayer: **"Our Father, who art in heaven, hallowed be Thy name. Thy kingdom come. Thy will be done on earth as it is in heaven. Give us this day our daily bread, and forgive us our trespasses, as we forgive those who trespass against us. And lead us not into temptation, but deliver us from evil. For Thine is the kingdom, and the power, and the glory forever and ever. Amen."**

    B. Today's place on the path: You can tell the Story as a love story, but you can also tell it as the Story of the human race growing up into maturity. Here's how to do it...

II. Today's lesson

    A. Listing human problems

    B. How we outgrow our problems through Christ

        1. Humanity outgrows violence

        2. Healing the family

        3. Growing up from poverty

    C. Falls, failures and the power of knowing the ending (Ps 2, Acts 4:23-31)

    D. Sharing with an unbeliever

ACTIVITIES

1. Remember the Ending. Have your students bring in a news article that reports some kind of pretty serious bad news. Have each student present their article briefly to the class (a few sentences is plenty). On the board, classify them all under broad headings—violence, family problems, poverty, war, disease, the cursed earth trying to kill us (fires, floods, hurricanes, etc.), and so on. When you're done, have someone read Revelation 21-22 aloud. Close with prayer, laying all these problems before God and thanking Him that in the end, they will all be resolved.

2. Journal Time: Do You Believe It? Have your students journal on the following questions.

- Do you really believe that every last one of the problems that now afflict the world will be resolved in the end? Every rape, kidnapping and murder will be set right, every environmental problem will be solved, every tyranny will be dissolved, every injustice dealt with? You don't have a hard time with any of that?

- Do you really believe that all will be well in the end? Why or why not?

Any of the things your students have trouble believing that God can resolve—have them take those things before God in prayer. They might pray something like this: "God, I don't see how You can resolve [problem]. I honestly don't think there's a way to make it right. Please tell me what you want me to know about this." Give them time to listen and see what God will say.

Lesson 6

EVALUATION

1. The understanding of history that was presented in this lesson—that things are slowly improving through the gospel over time—does that surprise you? Why or why not? **Obviously, these answers will be varied. Use the question as a diagnostic tool to evaluate how deeply the biblical Story has penetrated into your students.**

2. How violent was the pre-flood world, compared to our society? Give an example. **Far more violent. Lamech is just about the only specific example we have.**

3. How violent was the world Jesus was born into, compared to our society? Give an example. **Still far more violent. Examples include rampant banditry, the gladiatorial games, and Tiberius Caesar having prisoners tortured for his entertainment during dinner.**

4. Why is our society less violent? **Because we have 2,000 years of the gospel soaking into our society**

5. Name a way that a king a thousand years ago was poorer than most poor people in America today. **The king had to travel to escape the summer heat, if he could escape it at all. Today, even many of the poorest people have air conditioning. A king could only eat what was in season and could be transported to him by ship or wagon. We can go to the grocery store and buy fresh produce from around the world, in any season.**

6. Why did the apostles pray Psalm 2 when they were threatened and told not to preach Jesus? **Because Psalm 2 tells us what God thinks of earthly rulers trying to cast off His rule**

Peter and John healed a lame man in the name of Jesus; their lives were enriched by Jesus and they passed this richness on (Acts 3).

LESSON 7

Devotional Apologetics: Living in Beauty

NOTES TO THE TEACHER

In this lesson, we look at the same Story as in the last two lessons—because it's the only story there is. But this time we're going to come at it from an angle that traditional apologetic approaches rarely consider. Rather than giving reasonable answers, this lesson will focus on living a beautiful life. (Because the point of this lesson is to draw a sharp contrast between merely having the right answers *versus* having the right kind of life, we have not included an "Evaluation" section. We recommend that you do not quiz your students on this material.)

An activity for you
List five people you know who came to Christ as middle-schoolers or older. Reflect on what brought each of these people to Christ. Was it an argument? A personal tragedy? A significant person in their lives? Evangelistic preaching? A relative stranger who helped them in a time of desperate need?

Consider the implications of these peoples' stories for your teaching on apologetic interaction. It's fine to prepare your students to win arguments or talk a good game about the Christian life, but what we *do* is usually far more important than anything we could say. Part of your job in preparing your students for biblical apologetics—perhaps the most important part—is challenging them to live a life that will attract unbelievers to Christ.

Grasping the subject
Living a beautiful life can be a difficult concept for students to understand. If you're talking with

OVERVIEW

Being able to argue well is a valuable skill, and being able to tell the Christian Story well is an even more valuable skill. But when it comes to winning people to Christ, most people are far more persuaded by how Christians live than by what Christians say. Living beautifully is the best apologetic we can have.

SOURCE MATERIAL

- Matthew 10
- 2 Corinthians 4, 11
- N. D. Wilson, *Notes from the Tilt-a-Whirl* (audiobook available)
- N. D. Wilson, *Death by Living* (audiobook available)
- Rich Bledsoe, *Can Saul Alinsky Be Saved?*
- N. T. Wright, *Surprised by Hope*

a 30 or 40-year-old, you can say, "Look, some lives are just ugly, and others are beautiful." He's lived long enough and seen enough lives to know what you're talking about. Trying to help a 13-year-old see the same thing can be harder.

We suggest that you start with a middle school staple: a discussion of drug use. The subject is familiar territory, but we're going to put a bit of a different twist on it. Perhaps begin by showing one of the "Meth—Not Even Once" commercials. (They're all available on YouTube.) Then say something like this:

Devotional Apologetics

OBJECTIVES

The student will feel...

- perhaps a bit disappointed that talking a good game is not the only thing required to win people to Christ.
- empathy for people who make bad choices seeking good things.
- challenged to have a life that unbelievers will envy.

The student will understand...

- that most people want good things and a good life—which are supposed to be gifts from God—but they don't want to depend on God for these things.
- that trying to have God's good gifts without God leads to making bad choices and doesn't work in the end.
- that living as a Christian leads to The Good Life as a gift from God.
- that unbelievers will not be attracted to Christ if they can't see that Christians' lives are different from their own.
- that Jesus wants to make a visible difference in our lives, changing us from the heart outward.

The student will apply this understanding by...

- considering where his own life presents an attractive alternative to an unbeliever's life.
- asking God to help him develop the areas in his life that are not yet attractive to unbelievers.

If past years' statistics are any indication, at least 100,000 people are going to try meth for the first time this year. I bet not one of these people will look at a picture of "meth mouth" and say, "Yeah, that's what I want my teeth to look like!" I bet not one of them is looking forward to stealing to support a drug habit. I bet not one of them has these things in mind. So, what do they have in mind? Why do people do that? What are they looking for?

See if you can get a discussion going. What are people seeking? Common answers are...

- to impress their friends
- to have fun
- to forget their problems for a while
- to help them feel focused, strong, or confident

Write the answers down on the board—do everything you can to get a good list going.

Now, here's the twist: challenge your students to point at even one of the items on the board and say it's a bad thing. Your job is to defend every reason, if you can.

- Peer pressure: Is it a bad thing to want to get along with your friends?
- Trying to impress: Is there anything wrong with being admired? Isn't that a good thing?
- Having fun: Is it wrong to enjoy yourself?
- Forget your problems: Isn't it okay to rest, to de-stress? Didn't Jesus rest?
- Feeling focused, strong, or confident: Aren't these all good feelings?

The point here is that God made us to desire and respond to *good* things. In the new heavens and the new earth, when the kingdom of God has fully come, we will get along with our friends, people will think well of us, we will enjoy ourselves, we will get good rest, we will be focused, strong, and confident, etc. Even fallen as we are, we still respond to the desire for good things we are made to have. Nobody tries for a life of misery; we try for The Good Life, for a life that's beautiful, full of the things we will have in the kingdom of God. Nobody has to teach us to try for The Good Life. We do it naturally.

Author Steven Barnes tells the story of interviewing a murderer in a California prison. The man had strangled an old woman on the street with his bare hands. Surely, Barnes thought, he couldn't have wanted anything good. So he asked the man what happened. The murderer began to explain. He hadn't wanted to kill the lady; he just wanted to take her purse. She began to scream, and he was trying to get her to be quiet. So he choked her, but he held on too tight for too long, and she died. Barnes asked why he wanted her purse. "I needed money," the man said. Why? "I had to pay rent and buy some things." Why? "I needed to have my own place and have my life together" Why? What difference would it make? "If I had it together, people would respect me." What good is respect? "If people really respected me, and I didn't have to fight for respect all the time, then I could just...relax, you know? I could be myself."

Is it bad to want to be able to relax, to let your guard down? No. We were made to want—no, to *need*—to be ourselves, to be the people God made us to be without any kind of pretense.

As Christians, we must take the human desire for The Good Life seriously. As Christians, we also know that human beings are fallen. We are sinners by nature and by choice. How do we reconcile these two facts? Simple. The *way* we sin is not by being as bad as we can think to be (not usually, anyway). Almost nobody is that far gone. Mostly, we want good things, but don't want to have to say "Thank you" to God for them. Trying to avoid God, we take the wrong road to get the good things we want. The murderer Steven Barnes interviewed was at the end of a very long string of bad choices, all trying to get to a good place without God's help.

That is the effect of sin. The devil lies to us; the world lies to us. They both tell us we can take shortcuts, that bad choices will turn out to be fun or worth it somehow. And in our flesh, in our own sin, we want to believe it. There is a broad, easy way that leads to destruction, and a narrow way that leads to life. The narrow way is beautiful, but sometimes it's hard to find.

Living beautifully
When Jesus sent out the disciples to proclaim the gospel, He sent them out at the same time to *do* things: heal the sick, cast out demons, and so on (Matt 10:5-8, Luke 9:1-2, 10:9). Paul later reminded the Corinthians that he came to them in the demonstration of the Spirit and of power, not just with words (1 Cor 2:1-5). In Jesus' last teaching with His disciples before His arrest, Jesus told them that the world would recognize them as His disciples because of the love they would show each other (John 13:35). The common element throughout is simple: Christian witness must combine lip and life. What we do matters as much as what we say—sometimes more.

For example, Proverbs repeatedly commends diligence and condemns laziness, usually by pointing to the end results (see Prov 12:24, 13:4, 24:30-34). Hebrews makes a similar argument (Heb 13:7). It's not that we just live our lives and don't say a word. Rather, the words we say must not simply be elegant ideas; they must point to a visible reality in the world—*and we must live that reality*.

In using the pursuit of beauty as an evangelistic strategy, we win people to Christ by *inviting them into a beautiful life*. That doesn't happen if we only *talk* about a beautiful life. We must actually *have* a beautiful life to invite them into. We have to show them something worth seeing and let them experience it for themselves.

Which brings us to an important question: do you have a life that an unbeliever would want? When you invite someone to share your life, is there anything they will want to share? And if not, why not? The activities in this lesson are designed to address that issue.

Sacrifice?
We are so accustomed to thinking of the Christian life as a life of sacrifice that we sometimes forget the benefits. In the midst of being hated, we love, and we are loved. In the midst of the sorrow, we have joy. In the turmoil, we have peace and patience. In a brutal world, we are kind...and so on. A *lot* of people want a life characterized by these things, but they can't seem to find it. We know these things don't come from positive thinking or outside circumstances—they're the fruit of the Spirit.

It turns out these things do entail sacrifice, but there's a critical distinction here. *Faking* the fruit requires all the sacrifice, with none of the inner benefits. People who have lived as Christians for decades sometimes just walk away from the faith, seemingly overnight. "I just can't do it anymore," they say. But when someone walks away, it's not because they're repelled by the fruit of the Spirit. No one wakes up one morning and says, "I'm tired of experiencing love and joy in my heart all the time. I'm tired of having inner peace. I want some turmoil and misery!" What they're tired of is acting like a Christian without having the internal experience of life with the Spirit. They are tired of trying to mimic the fruit of the Spirit out of their own strength. If you behave in a loving manner while gritting your teeth, people may be grateful (if you can successfully conceal your displeasure), but you won't enjoy it. If you really do act out of love, then it will feel good, even if the sacrifice hurts at the same time.

You might make the point by having your students recall the last time they worked really hard on something, but really enjoyed it.

Resources
The four books listed in the resource section all highlight the beauty of the Christian Story and the beauty of living in the world as a Christian. We recommend them as an aid to beginning to think and live beautifully yourself, so that you can transmit the same patterns of life to your students.

Lesson 7

TEACHING OUTLINE

I. Introduction and review

   A. Teacher begins class by leading them in the Lord's Prayer: **"Our Father, who art in heaven, hallowed be Thy name. Thy kingdom come. Thy will be done on earth as it is in heaven. Give us this day our daily bread, and forgive us our trespasses, as we forgive those who trespass against us. And lead us not into temptation, but deliver us from evil. For Thine is the kingdom, and the power, and the glory forever and ever. Amen."**

   B. Today's place on the path: We know that the world is God's artwork and it conveys key truths about Him. We know that every human being, without exception, understands those truths deep down, but they suppress the truth. We know that all the facts worth knowing and the knowledge worth having come from Christ, and anybody who has knowledge, received it from Christ. And we know that it's our job as believers to expose the foolishness of unbelief without acting like fools ourselves. We can do this by sharing the Story of the world as a love story, or as a story where humanity grows up into maturity.

II. Today's lesson

   A. Wanting The Good Life

       1. Meth example

       2. What are people looking for?

       3. We always take a wrong turn.

   B. Christian witness must be lip and life.

   C. Activities

       1. Self-evaluation

       2. Prayer

ACTIVITIES

1. Self-Evaluation. Challenge your students with the following list of questions (in plain text). We recommend that you talk a little about each question along the lines of the bold print below, so that they understand the questions well. The students don't need to answer every question; just have each student choose whichever one jumps out at him.

- How do I handle it when I don't get my way? **Taking it gracefully when things don't go well is a mark of maturity. Everybody knows that things aren't going to go their way sometimes. If you can show your students a way to handle it well when things don't go their way, that is very attractive to unbelievers.**

- Do I get jealous when someone has more (money, popularity, talent, good looks, better grades, etc.) than I do? **Contentment is an important aspect of the Christian life. We say that happiness does not depend on those things, but if we can** show **unbelievers this truth, then we have something really attractive.**
- How often am I really at peace? **To some extent, this will depend on personality—some people are just more laid-back and some are more anxious. But we are all called to exhibit the Spirit's fruit, and that means a life of inner peace.**
- What does it take to make me happy? Unhappy? **If your uncle dies, and you're sad, that's normal and natural, and no unbeliever looks at that and thinks, "Why would I want to live like that?" However, if your hair spray doesn't work the way you want and that ruins your whole day... that's another thing. On the flip side, are you able to be happy about the small things, or does it take something really big to make you smile?**
- How do I handle my unhappiness? **People's distractions of choice vary—video games, friends, chocolate, sex, heroin—but the dynamics are the same. Do you distract yourself, wallow in misery, throw a tantrum, make everyone around you miserable? Any unbeliever can do these things. Or do you take it gracefully in a way that makes an unbeliever wonder how you do that?**
- When was the last time I was really grateful for something? **Gratitude has a direct influence on our happiness. If we're not often grateful, then we will not be happy.**
- When my friends are happy/sad, can I be happy/sad with them? **Because we love our neighbors, Christians should be able to enter into their happiness (or sadness) with them. The ability to share in others' lives is one of the critical building blocks for quality relationships.**
- Does anybody else want the kind of relationship I have with (God, friends, parents, siblings, teachers, coaches, etc.)? **If nobody would look at your relationships and see anything they wish they had, then your relationships are broken.**
- Do I praise God no matter what's happening? **Genuine, heartfelt praise in difficult times is a mystery to the world.**
- What's so great about being a Christian *right now*? **"I'm going to heaven when I die" doesn't count. It's important, but that's not the question. The question is: what difference does it make today? How is your life different from an unbeliever's?**

2. Prayer Activity. Have your students read 2 Corinthians 11:24-28, which is a description of Paul's life. Everywhere he went, people wanted to kill him. But everywhere he went, people also wanted to be like him—they wanted what he had, and they came to Christ so they could have it too. Obviously, they were not attracted to Paul's external circumstances; it was how Paul handled it all that was attractive (see 2 Cor 4:8-9). With that in mind, have your students consider these questions:

- Who would want my life? Do I have a life that an unbeliever would want? **If thinking about all of life is a bit too daunting, go on to the next question.**
- Is there a *part* of my life I could invite an unbelieving friend into? **Where could I share my life with an unbeliever and show him something that God is doing?**
- What parts of my life are no different from an unbeliever's? **Once you've identified those areas, take your list before God and ask the next question.**
- Ask God, "Which area of my life do You want me to focus on right now?" **As with any time you seek to hear God, take some time with the question on your own and see what God will bring to mind, but also seek out godly counsel.**
- Ask God, "What do You want this area of my life to look like? And how do I get there?" **The answer may involve some surprises. Again, seek to hear God yourself, but also seek out godly counsel. God speaks through His people and His Word as well as directly to you.**

www.ingramcontent.com/pod-product-compliance
Lightning Source LLC
Chambersburg PA
CBHW081339080526
44588CB00017B/2682